CW00645830

DECADENCE

DECADENCE

A Literary Anthology

Selected by Jon Crabb

CONTENTS

Introduction

I love this word decadence, all shimmering in purple and gold. It suggests
the subtle thoughts of ultimate civilization, a high literary culture, a soul
capable of intense pleasures. It throws off bursts of fire and the sparkle
of precious stones. It is redolent of the rouge of courtesans, the games of the
circus, the panting of the gladiators, the spring of wild beasts,
the consuming in flames of races exhausted by their capacity for
sensation, as the tramp of an invading army sounds.
Paul Verlaine

The word *luxury* has the same root as lechery, lust and lasciviousness. By
the archaic definition, luxury was seen as something to be shunned, hidden
away, shamefully resisted. To indulge was to rebel. To openly luxuriate in
sensation (whether vice or virtue) was to be *decadent*.

Standing at the threshold of the twentieth century, Janus-faced, with
a foot in both the old and the new, the 1890s were a time of social change,
moral outcry, and fierce artistic debate throughout Europe. In the world of
arts and letters, we can say with confidence that something was most
definitely astir. New forms of artistic expression were blossoming in
London around such figures as Oscar Wilde, Aubrey Beardsley, Max
Beerbohm, Ernest Dowson and Arthur Symons, who in turn took their cue
from the earlier French writers Charles Baudelaire, J. K. Huysmans,
Théophile Gautier and Paul Verlaine. Under the maxim 'Art for Art's
Sake' they defied moral convention and pursued the limits of sensation
and indulgence, wilfully transgressing Victorian respectability along the
way. Early in the decade, a host of boundary-pushing artists were criticised
by Max Nordau in an infamous essay called *Degeneration* (1892), in which
he found evidence of madness in the works of the Impressionists, Charles
Baudelaire, Henrik Ibsen, Leo Tolstoy, Émile Zola and Oscar Wilde. They
were in turn defended in essays such as A. E. Hake's *Regeneration: A Reply*
to Max Nordau and *The Sanity of Art* by George Bernard Shaw. In what

was increasingly set up as cultural warfare by those involved, the groups that made up this strange new generation embraced their identities as brave *Artists* and rallied against the *Philistines*. W. B. Yeats wrote that they 'Delighted in enemies and in everything else that had an heroic aire'. The other side was only too happy to play the same game, and a journalist from the *Westminster Gazette* named J. A. Spender took up the pen-name 'The Philistine', as he retaliated against the 'New Hedonism', the 'New Woman', the 'New Art' and any other affront to common decency that he could find. Both sides drew up their forces and filled the opinion pages of the newspapers. Arthur Symons wrote that 'Decadence' was 'either hurled as a reproach or hurled back as a defiance'.

For a while it was all good clean fun that gave young men something to proselytise, old men something to condemn, and the press something to print. What had begun in Paris a couple of decades previously was reaching a joyous zenith in London. But, as quickly as it began, the mood darkened. In 1895, after a widely publicised and scandalous court case, Oscar Wilde was condemned to hard labour in prison for 'immorality' after his relationships with other men came to light. It was a symbolic event that crystallised prevailing Victorian attitudes at the time. A gleeful popular press ran headlines such as 'The Aesthetic Cult, in the Nasty form, is Over' (*News of the World*, 26 May 1895). The newly translated Nordau was widely read, but the Aesthetic Cult was not quite over yet. A host of 'little magazines', such as the *Yellow Book*, the *Savoy*, the *Dial*, the *Hobby Horse* and the *Pagan Review*, as well as brave publishers like Leonard Smithers and John Lane with his *Keynotes* series, published decadent, contentious or subversive material throughout the 1890s. Space prevents a full discussion of the momentous impact these publications had, but a host of rebellious thinkers – among them aesthetes, early feminists, occultists and a rapidly emerging gay community – was finding a voice and reaching an audience. What was condemned as degeneration could be more properly termed rebirth or renewal. Even among the self-consciously decadent, for whom the mantle was worn with pride, there was a seriousness to their investigations of previously taboo areas. Art and luxury were pursued with an almost spiritual fervour.

This illustrated anthology is separated into chapters on the major preoccupations of decadence – namely Artifice, Intoxication, Spirituality and Death. The selections include some of the finest examples of decadent prose and poetry, as well as lesser-known pieces, extracts from theoretical texts, criticism and parody. The pursuit of the exotic had its roots in the Gothic literature of the eighteenth century, written by such proto-decadents as William Beckford, and a number of texts that inspired the Decadent movement of the *fin de siècle* are featured. The seminal descriptions of drug use in *Confessions of An English Opium-Eater* encouraged a generation to seek flights of fancy in oblivion. Extracts from Walter Pater contextualise aesthetic principles, and extracts from Max Nordau's *Degeneration* illustrate just how much controversy it all caused. This being the British Library's anthology of decadent literature, the focus is necessarily on its British exponents, but some of the strangest and most exquisite decadent writing is in fact French... As one journeys through the following selections it will become obvious how much the British writers idealised France and sought to live *la vie Parisienne*, even if they happened to be stuck on the wrong side of the Channel. But this merely added to the peculiar, magical atmosphere of 1890s London. It was as much a state of mind as an actual time and place.

It is rather hard not to romanticise the decadents as the 'tragic generation' when, as John Betjeman pointed out, 'this was the world which ended in prison and disgrace for Wilde, suicide for Crackenthorpe and John Davidson, premature death for Beardsley, Dowson and Lionel Johnson, religion for some, drink and drugs for others, temporary or permanent oblivion for many more'. Arthur Symons avoided an early death, but suffered a nervous breakdown and bout of insanity in 1908 that ended his career. Exercising a slightly selective memory, W. B. Yeats wrote that 'in 1900 everybody got down off his stilts; henceforth nobody drank absinthe with his black coffee; nobody went mad; nobody committed suicide; nobody joined the Catholic church; or if they did I have forgotten'. He had forgotten. A few who survived that meridian succumbed to one or all of those things within the next decade. They were truly the first generation to be so *entirely* overcome by death, intoxication and madness.

In the *Proverbs of Hell*, Blake wrote, 'The road of excess leads to the palace of wisdom'. Whilst many decadents took those words to heart, their fates are a painful reminder that the route is a dangerous one and genius is not always met with health and happiness. Often, these fascinating figures lived true to their art and led lives more eccentric and captivating than anything they created. As a key part of the decadent myth, short biographies can be found at the back of this anthology.

Jon Crabb, Editor,
British Library Publishing

1

An Æsthetical Instinct – PROPHETS

One should always be a little improbable.
Oscar Wilde

After all, a little charlatanry is permitted to genius.
It is like the paint on the cheeks of a naturally
beautiful woman, a new condition of the mind.
Charles Baudelaire

Extracts from *Recollections of the Late William Beckford of Fonthill, Wilts; and Lansdown, Bath* (1893)

HENRY VENN LANSDOWN

The extraordinary William Beckford was a decadent before his time. It would not be much of an overstatement to claim that the Decadent movement in Britain began with him. Fabulously wealthy, yet restless and unhappy, he retreated into a world of literature and objets d'art. *His only novel,* Vathek, *served as a direct inspiration to J. K. Huysmans's* À Rebours. *Beckford once said: 'Some people drink to forget their unhappiness. I do not drink, I build.' Fonthill Abbey was the enormous Gothic spectacle that resulted from his peculiar mania. The tower, 300ft tall, collapsed several times, and the entire abbey was eventually demolished. The extracts printed here are from a collection of letters written by Henry Venn Lansdown to his daughter, describing several encounters with the aging Beckford in a new house, and a visit to the ruins of Fonthill. They vividly evoke the brilliance of the man and his follies.*

Bath, August 21, 1838

My Dear Charlotte, – I have this day seen such an astonishing assemblage of works of art, so numerous and of so surprisingly rare a description that I am literally what Lord Byron calls 'Dazzled and drunk with beauty.' I feel so bewildered from beholding the rapid succession of some of the very finest productions of the great masters that the attempt to describe them seems an impossible task; however, I will make an effort.

The collection of which I speak is that of Mr. Beckford, at his house in Lansdown-crescent. Besides all this I have this day been introduced to that extraordinary man, the author of 'Vathek' and 'Italy,' the builder of Fonthill, the contemporary of the mighty and departed dead, the pupil of Mozart; in fact, to the formidable and inaccessible Vathek himself! I have many times passed the house, and longed to see its contents, and often have I wondered how a building with so plain and unostentatious an exterior could suit the reception of the works it contains, and the residence of so magnificent a personage.

I first called by appointment on his ingenious architect, Mr. Goodridge (to whom I am indebted for this distinguished favour), and he accompanied me to the house, which we reached at half-past twelve o'clock. We were shown upstairs, passing many fine family pictures, and were ushered into the neat library, where Mr. Beckford was waiting to receive us. I confess I did at first feel somewhat embarrassed, but a lovely spaniel ran playfully towards us, licking our hands in the most affectionate and hospitable manner; 'You are welcome' was the silent language. I assure you I judge much, and often truly, of the character of individuals from the deportment of their favourite dogs. I often find them exactly indicative of their master's disposition. When you are attacked by snarling, waspish curs is it at all wonderful if you find them an echo of the proprietor? But this beautiful animal reassured me, and gave me instantly a favourable idea of its master. My astonishment was great at the spaciousness of the room, which had in length a magnificent and palatial effect, nor did I immediately discover the cause of its apparent grandeur. It opens into the gallery built over the arch connecting the two houses, at the end of which an immense mirror reflects the two apartments. The effect is most illusive, nor should I have guessed the truth had I not seen the reflection of my own figure in the glass.

The library, which is the whole length of the first house, cannot be much less than fifty feet long. It has on one side five lofty windows, the gallery having three on the same side. You have the light streaming through eight consecutive openings; these openings, with their crimson curtains, doubled by the reflection, produce a most charming perspective. From the ceiling hangs a splendid ormolu chandelier, the floor is covered with a Persian carpet (brought I believe from Portugal), so sumptuous that one is afraid to walk on it, and a noble mosaic table of Florentine marble, bought in at an immense price at Fonthill, is in the centre of the room. Several rows of the rarest books cover the lower part of the walls, and above them) hang many fine portraits, which Mr. Beckford immediately, without losing any time in compliments, began to show us and describe.

First we were shown a portrait by de Vos of Grotius; next to it one of Rembrandt, painted by himself. 'You see,' said Mr. Beckford, 'that he is trying to assume an air of dignity not natural to him, by throwing back his head, but this attempt at the dignified is neutralized by the expression of the eyes, which have rather too much of sly humour for the character which he wishes to give himself.' To praise individual pictures seems useless when everyone you meet has excellencies peculiar to itself; in fact, whatever our ideas of the great masters may be, and we certainly do gain from prints and pictures a tolerable idea of their style and different beauties (and I have myself seen the Louvre and many celebrated pictures) there is in Mr. Beckford's *chef d'oeuvres* something still more lovely than our imagination, than our expectation. I speak not now of the St. Catherine, The Claud [*sic*], The Titian, &c., but all the pictures, whether historical, landscape, or low life, have this unique character of excellence. You look at a picture. You are sure it is by Gaspar, but you never saw one of Poussin's that had such an exquisite tone of colour, so fresh and with such free and brilliant execution.

There really seems some charm, some magic in the walls, so great is the similarity of colouring in these *chefs d'oeuvres*, the clear, the subdued, the pearly tints, a variety of delicious colour, and none of the dirty hues you see in mediocre old paintings.

Over the sofa is a constellation of beauties which we merely glanced at as we passed, but which I hope another day to examine. They are some of the rarest specimens by G. Poussin, Wouvermans, Berghem, Van Huysum, Polemberg, and others. On a small table was placed an elegantly cut caraffe of carnations of every variety of colour that you can possibly imagine. There is nothing in which Mr. Beckford is more choice than in his bouquets. At every season the rarest living flowers adorn the house.

Next to the dining room is a small salon, which we now entered. Here is a noble drawing by Turner of the Abbey, according to a plan proposed, but never carried out. The tower is conical, and would have been even higher than the one that was completed. 'I have seen,' I said, 'a fine drawing of Fonthill by Turner, originally in your possession, but now belonging to Mr. Allnutt, of Clapham. It is prodigiously fine. The scenery there must be magnificent. The hills and beautiful lake in the drawing give one an idea of Cumberland.' 'It is a very fine drawing, but rather too poetical, too ideal, even for Fonthill. The scenery there is certainly beautiful, but Turner took such liberties with it that he entirely destroyed the portraiture, the locality of the spot. That was the reason I parted with it. There were originally six drawings of the Abbey; three were disposed of at the sale, and I still have the remaining ones.' 'Are they going to rebuild the tower, sir? for when I was last in London, Papworth, the architect, was gone down to Fonthill to do something there.' 'Impossible,' he said, unless it were to be made a national affair, which indeed is not very likely. It would cost at least £100,000 to restore it. But what can Papworth have done there? It must I should think be something to the pavilion. I assure you I had no idea of parting with Fonthill till Farquhar made me the offer. I wished to purge it, to get rid of a great many things I did not want, but as to the building itself I had no more notion of selling it than you have (turning to his architect) of parting with anything, with – with the clothes you have on.

On the chimney piece, protected by a glass, is a precious Japan vase. We examined it for some time under its envelope. It seemed to me (for I know nothing of Japan work) a bronze vessel, richly and most elaborately chased, and I could not help joining in the praises due to its exquisite finish. Mr. Beckford took off the glass, and desired me to take it to the window. 'I am really afraid to touch it,' said I, but he forced it into my hands. I prepared them to receive a massive and (as it seemed to me) very weighty vessel, when lo it proved as light as a feather. We were afterwards shown another Japan vase, the exterior of which exactly resembled the Pompeian designs, elegant scrolls, delicate tracery of blue, red, green, &c. These colours strongly opposed as in the remains of paintings at Pompeii. Here are some other precious little pictures, a small Gerard Dow, a Watteau, a Moucheron, and a Polemberg. He merely noticed them, and then led us into the next room.

A noble library. It is an elegant and charming apartment, very chastely ornamented. Here are no pictures; it is devoted entirely to books and ponderous folios of the most rare and precious engravings. The sides of the library are adorned by Scagliola pilasters and arched recesses, which contain the books. The interstices between the arches and the ceiling are painted in imitation of marble, so extremely like that though they touch the Scagliola it is next to impossible to distinguish any difference. The ceiling is belted across and enriched with bands of Grecian tracery in relief, delicately painted and slightly touched with gold. On the walls are some gilded ornaments, enough to give to the whole richness of effect without heaviness. Between the windows is what I suppose may be termed a table, composed of an enormous slab of the rarest marble, supported by elegantly cast bronze legs. Over this a small cabinet (manufactured in Bath from drawings by Mr. Goodridge) full of extremely small books; it is carved in oak in the most elaborate manner. The fireplace, of Devonshire marble, is perfect in design and in its adaptation to the rest of the room; in fact, everything in this lovely chamber is in unison, everything soft, quiet, and subdued.

New wonders awaited me. Next to the library is a sort of vestibule leading to a staircase, which from its mysterious and crimson light, rich draperies, and latticed doors seemed to be the sanctum sanctorum of a heathen temple. To the left a long passage, whose termination not being seen allowed the imagination full play, led for aught I know to the Fortress of Akerman, to the Montagne du Caf or to the Halls of Argenti. *Ou sout peintes toutes les createures raissonables, et les animaux qui ont habité la terre.*

To the right two latticed doors, reminding you of Grand Cairo or Persepolis, ingeniously conceal the commonplace entrance from the Crescent. The singular and harmonious light of this mysterious vestibule is produced by crimson silk strained over the fanlight of the outer door. 'This place,' I observed, 'puts one in mind of the Hall of Eblis.' 'You are quite right,' he observed, 'this is unquestionably the Hall of Eblis.' 'Those latticed doors,' I continued, 'seem to lead to the small apartment where the three princes, Alasi, Barkiarokh, and Kalilah, related to Vathek and Nouronchar their adventures.' He seemed amused at my observations, and said, 'Then you have read "Vathek." How do you like it?' 'Vastly. I read it in English many years ago, but never in French.' 'Then read it in French,' said Mr. Beckford. 'The French edition is much finer than the English.'

October 28, 1844

The evening was most lovely. A soft haze had prevailed the whole afternoon, and as there was still an hour's daylight I determined on instantly visiting the ruins. Just without the sacred enclosure that once prevented all intrusion to this mysterious solitude is the lovely little village of Fonthill Gifford; its charming cottages, with their neat gardens and blooming roses, are a perfect epitome of English rusticity. A padlocked gate admits the visitor within the barrier; a steep road, but gently winding so as to make access easy, leads you to the bill, where once stood 'the gem and the wonder of earth.'

The road is broad and entirely arched by trees. Emerging suddenly from their covert an astonishing assemblage of ruins comes into view. Before you stands the magnificent eastern transept with its two beautiful octangular towers, still rising to the height of 120 feet, but roofless and desolate; the three stately windows, 60 feet high, as open to the sky as Glastonbury Abbey; in the rooms once adorned with choicest paintings and rarities trees are growing. Oh what a scene of desolation! What the noble poet said of 'Vathek's' residence in Portugal we may now literally say of Fonthill.

> Here grown weeds a passage scarce allow
> To halls deserted, portals gaping wide.
> Fresh lessons, ye thinking bosoms, how
> Vain are the pleasures by earth supplied,
> Swept into wrecks anon by Time's ungentle tide.

Of all desolate scenes there are none so desolate as those which we now see as ruins, and which were lately the abode of splendour and magnificence. Ruins that have been such for ages, whose tenants have long since been swept away, recall ideas of persons and times so far back that we have no sympathy with them at all; but if you wish for a sight of all that is melancholy, all that is desolate, visit a modern ruin. We passed through briars and brambles into the great octagon. Straight before us stands the western doorway of the noble entrance hall; but where is its oaken roof, with its proud heraldic emblazonments, where its lofty painted windows, where its ponderous doors, more than 30 feet high? The cross still remains above, as if symbolical that religion triumphs over all, and St. Anthony still holds out his right hand as if to protect the sylvan and mute inhabitants of these groves that here once found secure shelter from the cruel gun and still more cruel dog. But he is tottering in his niche, and when the wind is high is seen to rock, as if his reign were drawing to a close.

Of the noble octagon but two sides remain. Looking up, but at such an amazing elevation that it makes one's neck ache, still are seen two windows of the four nunneries that adorned its unique and unrivalled circuit. And what is more wonderful than all, the noble organ screen, designed by 'Vathek' himself, has still survived; its gilded lattices, though exposed for twenty years to the 'pelting of the pitiless storm,' yet glitter in the last rays of the setting sun.

Extract from *The History of the Caliph Vathek* (1786)

WILLIAM BECKFORD

A paean to excess – in art, in music, in food, in flesh, in theology – the Caliph Vathek is partly William Beckford himself, although even he could not aspire to the magnificence of his fictional anti-hero.

Vathek, ninth Caliph of the race of the Abassides, was the son of Motassem, and the grandson of Haroun Al Raschid. From an early accession to the throne, and the talents he possessed to adorn it, his subjects were induced to expect that his reign would be long and happy. His figure was pleasing and majestic; but when he was angry one of his eyes became so terrible that no person could bear to behold it, and the wretch upon whom it was fixed instantly fell backward, and sometimes expired. For fear, however, of depopulating his dominions and making his palace desolate he but rarely gave way to his anger.

Being much addicted to women and the pleasures of the table, he sought by his affability to procure agreeable companions; and he succeeded the better as his generosity was unbounded, and his indulgences unrestrained, for he was by no means scrupulous, nor did he think with the Caliph Omar Ben Abdalaziz that it was necessary to make a hell of this world to enjoy Paradise in the next.

He surpassed in magnificence all his predecessors. The palace of Alkoremmi, which his father Motassem had erected on the hill of Pied Horses, and which commanded the whole city of Samarah, was in his idea far too scanty; he added therefore five wings, or rather other palaces, which he destined for the particular gratification of each of his senses.

In the first of these were tables continually covered with the most exquisite dainties, which were supplied both by night and by day, according to their constant consumption, whilst the most delicious wines and the choicest cordials flowed forth from a hundred fountains that were never exhausted. This palace was called 'The Eternal or Unsatiating Banquet.'

The second was styled 'The Temple of Melody, or the Nectar of the Soul.' It was inhabited by the most skilful musicians and admired poets of the time, who not only displayed their talents within, but, dispersing in bands without, caused every surrounding scene to reverberate their songs, which were continually varied in the most delightful succession.

The palace named 'The Delight of the Eyes, or the Support of Memory' was one entire enchantment. Rarities collected from every corner of the earth were there found in such profusion as to dazzle and confound, but for the order in which they were arranged. One gallery exhibited the pictures of the celebrated Mani, and statues that seemed to be alive. Here a well-managed perspective attracted the sight; there the magic of optics agreeably deceived it; whilst the naturalist on his part exhibited, in their several classes, the various gifts that Heaven had bestowed on our globe. In a word, Vathek omitted nothing in this palace that might gratify the curiosity of those who resorted to it, although he was not able to satisfy his own, for he was of all men the most curious.

'The Palace of Perfumes,' which was termed likewise 'The Incentive to Pleasure,' consisted of various halls, where the different perfumes which the earth produces were kept perpetually burning in censers of gold. Flambeaux and aromatic lamps were here lighted in open day. But the too powerful effects of this agreeable delirium might be avoided by descending into an immense garden, where an assemblage of every fragrant flower diffused through the air the purest odours.

The fifth palace, denominated 'The Retreat of Joy, or the Dangerous,' was frequented by troops of young females beautiful as the houris and not less seducing, who never failed to receive with caresses all whom the Caliph allowed to approach them; for he was by no means disposed to be jealous, as his own women were secluded within the palace he inhabited himself.

Notwithstanding the sensuality in which Vathek indulged, he experienced no abatement in the love of his people, who thought that a sovereign immersed in pleasure was not less tolerable to his subjects than one that employed himself in creating them foes. But the unquiet and impetuous disposition of the Caliph would not allow him to rest there; he had studied so much for his amusement in the lifetime of his father as to acquire a great deal of knowledge, though not a sufficiency to satisfy himself; for he wished to know everything, even sciences that did not exist. He was fond of engaging in disputes with the learned, but liked them not to push their opposition with warmth; he stopped the mouths of those with presents whose mouths could be stopped, whilst others, whom his liberality was unable to subdue, he sent to prison to cool their blood: a remedy that often succeeded.

Vathek discovered also a predilection for theological controversy, but it was not with the orthodox that he usually held. By this means he induced the zealots to oppose him, and then persecuted them in return; for he resolved at any rate to have reason on his side.

The great prophet Mahomet, whose vicars the caliphs are, beheld with indignation from his abode in the seventh heaven the irreligious conduct of such a vicegerent. 'Let us leave him to himself,' said he to the Genii, who are always ready to receive his commands; 'let us see to what lengths his folly and impiety will carry him; if he run into excess we shall know how to chastise him.'

Extract from *Confessions of an English Opium-Eater* (1821)

THOMAS DE QUINCEY

De Quincey's drug-induced reverie is remarkable, not just for its dazzling imagery but for the horrified fascination with the East it reveals. This is a sinister yet gorgeous piece of writing.

May 1818

The Malay has been a fearful enemy for months. I have been every night, through his means, transported into Asiatic scenes. I know not whether others share in my feelings on this point; but I have often thought that if I were compelled to forego England, and to live in China, and among Chinese manners and modes of life and scenery, I should go mad. The causes of my horror lie deep, and some of them must be common to others. Southern Asia in general is the seat of awful images and associations. As the cradle of the human race, it would alone have a dim and reverential feeling connected with it. But there are other reasons. No man can pretend that the wild, barbarous, and capricious superstitions of Africa, or of savage tribes elsewhere, affect him in the way that he is affected by the ancient, monumental, cruel, and elaborate religions of Indostan, &c. The mere antiquity of Asiatic things, of their institutions, histories, modes of faith, &c., is so impressive, that to me the vast age of the race and name overpowers the sense of youth in the individual. A young Chinese seems to me an antediluvian man renewed. Even Englishmen, though not bred in any knowledge of such institutions, cannot but shudder at the mystic sublimity of *castes* that have flowed apart, and refused to mix, through such immemorial tracts of time; nor can any man fail to be awed by the names of the Ganges or the Euphrates. It contributes much to these feelings that southern Asia is, and has been for thousands of years, the part of the earth most swarming with human life, the great *officina gentium*.

Man is a weed in those regions. The vast empires also in which the enormous population of Asia has always been cast, give a further sublimity to the feelings associated with all Oriental names or images. In China, over and above what it has in common with the rest of southern Asia, I am terrified by the modes of life, by the manners, and the barrier of utter abhorrence and want of sympathy placed between us by feelings deeper than I can analyse. I could sooner live with lunatics or brute animals. All this, and much more than I can say or have time to say, the reader must enter into before he can comprehend the unimaginable horror which these dreams of Oriental imagery and mythological tortures impressed upon me. Under the connecting feeling of tropical heat and vertical sunlights I brought together all creatures, birds, beasts, reptiles, all trees and plants, usages and appearances, that are found in all tropical regions, and assembled them together in China or Indostan. From kindred feelings, I soon brought Egypt and all her gods under the same law. I was stared at, hooted at, grinned at, chattered at, by monkeys, by parroquets, by cockatoos. I ran into pagodas, and was fixed for centuries at the summit or in secret rooms: I was the idol; I was the priest; I was worshipped; I was sacrificed. I fled from the wrath of Brama through all the forests of Asia: Vishnu hated me: Seeva laid wait for me. I came suddenly upon Isis and Osiris: I had done a deed, they said, which the ibis and the crocodile trembled at. I was buried for a thousand years in stone coffins, with mummies and sphynxes, in narrow chambers at the heart of eternal pyramids. I was kissed, with cancerous kisses, by crocodiles; and laid, confounded with all unutterable slimy things, amongst reeds and Nilotic mud.

I thus give the reader some slight abstraction of my Oriental dreams, which always filled me with such amazement at the monstrous scenery that horror seemed absorbed for a while in sheer astonishment. Sooner or later came a reflux of feeling that swallowed up the astonishment, and left me not so much in terror as in hatred and abomination of what I saw. Over every form, and threat, and punishment, and dim sightless incarceration, brooded a sense of eternity and infinity that drove me into an oppression as of madness. Into these dreams only it was, with one or two slight exceptions, that any circumstances of physical horror entered. All before had been moral and spiritual terrors. But here the main agents were ugly birds, or snakes, or crocodiles; especially the last. The cursed crocodile became to me the object of more horror than almost all the rest. I was compelled to live with him, and (as was always the case almost in my dreams) for centuries. I escaped sometimes, and found myself in Chinese houses, with cane tables, &c. All the feet of the tables, sofas, &c., soon became instinct with life: the abominable head of the crocodile, and his leering eyes, looked out at me, multiplied into a thousand repetitions; and I stood loathing and fascinated. And so often did this hideous reptile haunt my dreams that many times the very same dream was broken up in the very same way: I heard gentle voices speaking to me (I hear everything when I am sleeping), and instantly I awoke. It was broad noon, and my children were standing, hand in hand, at my bedside – come to show me their coloured shoes, or new frocks, or to let me see them dressed for going out. I protest that so awful was the transition from the damned crocodile, and the other unutterable monsters and abortions of my dreams, to the sight of innocent *human* natures and of infancy, that in the mighty and sudden revulsion of mind I wept, and could not forbear it, as I kissed their faces.

'Pelham's Maxims' from *Pelham: Or the Adventures of a Gentleman* (1828)

EDWARD BULWER-LYTTON

A taste for clothes usually went with a taste for art and literature, and many key figures of the fin de siècle *were recognisable by a particular sartorial quirk or extravagance. To break the rules, one must know the rules. These maxims for the dapper gentleman lack the perversity of a truly decadent text, but they foreshadow the aphorisms of Oscar Wilde and contain a wonderfully understated dry humour.*

1.) Do not require your dress so much to fit, as to adorn you. Nature is not to be copied, but to be exalted by art. Apelles blamed Protogenes for being too natural.

2.) Never in your dress altogether desert that taste which is general. The world considers eccentricity in great things, genius; in small things, folly.

3.) Always remember that you dress to fascinate others, not yourself.

4.) Keep your mind free from all violent affections at the hour of the toilet. A philosophical serenity is perfectly necessary to success. Helvetius says justly, that our errors arise from our passions.

5.) Remember that none but those whose courage is unquestionable, can venture to be effeminate. It was only in the field that the Lacedemonians were accustomed to use perfumes and curl their hair.

6.) Never let the finery of chains and rings seem your own choice; that which naturally belongs to women should appear only worn for their sake. We dignify foppery, when we invest it with a sentiment.

7.) To win the affection of your mistress, appear negligent in your costume – to preserve it, assiduous: the first is a sign of the passion of love; the second, of its respect.

8.) A man must be a profound calculator to be a consummate dresser.

One must not dress the same, whether one goes to a minister or a mistress; an avaricious uncle, or an ostentatious cousin: there is no diplomacy more subtle than that of dress.

9.)   Is the great man whom you would conciliate a coxcomb? – go to him in a waistcoat like his own. 'Imitation,' says the author of Lacon, 'is the sincerest flattery.'

10.) The handsome may be shewy in dress, the plain should study to be unexceptionable; just as in great men we look for something to admire – in ordinary men we ask for nothing to forgive.

11.) There is a study of dress for the aged, as well as for the young. Inattention is no less indecorous in one than in the other; we may distinguish the taste appropriate to each, by the reflection that youth is made to be loved-age, to be respected.

12.) A fool may dress gaudily, but a fool cannot dress well – for to dress well requires judgment; and Rochefaucault says with truth, 'On est quelquefois un sot avec de l'esprit, mais on ne lest jamais avec du jugement.'

13.) There may be more pathos in the fall of a collar, or the curl of a lock, than the shallow think for. Should we be so apt as we are now to compassionate the misfortunes, and to forgive the insincerity of Charles I, if his pictures had pourtrayed him in a bob wig and a pigtail? Vandyke was a greater sophist than Hume.

14.) The most graceful principle of dress is neatness – the most vulgar is preciseness.

15.) Dress contains the two codes of morality – private and public. Attention is the duty we owe to others – cleanliness that which we owe to ourselves.

16.) Dress so that it may never be said of you 'What a well dressed man!' – but, 'What a gentlemanlike man!'

17.) Avoid many colours; and seek, by some one prevalent and quiet tint, to sober down the others. Apelles used only four colours, and always subdued those which were more florid, by a darkening varnish.

18.) Nothing is superficial to a deep observer! It is in trifles that the mind betrays itself. 'In what part of that letter,' said a king to the wisest of living diplomatists, 'did you discover irresolution?' – 'In its ns and gs!' was the answer.

19.) A very benevolent man will never shock the feelings of others, by an excess either of inattention or display; you may doubt, therefore, the philanthropy both of a sloven and a fop.

20.) There is an indifference to please in a stocking down at heel – but there may be a malevolence in a diamond ring.

21.) Inventions in dressing should resemble Addison's definition of fine writing, and consists of 'refinements which are natural, without being obvious.'

22.) He who esteems trifles for themselves, is a trifler – he who esteems them for the conclusions to be drawn from them, or the advantage to which they can be put, is a philosopher.

Extract from *À Rebours* (1884)

J. K. HUYSMANS

This is the decadent text par excellence. Later British acolytes all emulated
À Rebours *to some extent. It took great restraint to choose only one extract*
for this anthology, but this particular section is a perfect mixture of
theatricality, technical detail, morbid humour and subversive eroticism. The
'sensitive' protagonist describes a funeral feast held to mark the death of his
potency. Sexual vitality is subsumed and reborn as sensual extravagance.

In the days when Des Esseintes still deemed it incumbent on him to play
the eccentric, he had also installed strange and elaborate dispositions of
furniture and fittings, partitioning off his salon into a series of niches,
each differently hung and carpeted, and each harmonizing in a subtle
likeness by a more or less vague similarity of tints, gay or sombre, refined
or barbaric, with the special character of the Latin and French books he
loved. He would then settle himself down to read in whichever of these
recesses displayed in its scheme of decoration the closest correspondence
with the intimate essence of the particular book his caprice of the moment
led him to peruse.

Last fancy of all, he had prepared a lofty hall in which to receive his
tradesmen. These would march in, take seats side by side in a row of
church stalls; then he would mount an imposing pulpit and preach them a
sermon on dandyism, adjuring his bookmakers and tailors to conform with
the most scrupulous fidelity to his commandments in the matter of cut
and fashion, threatening them with the penalty of pecuniary
excommunication if they failed to follow out to the letter the instructions
embodied in his monitories and bulls.

He won a great reputation as an eccentric – a reputation he crowned
by adopting a costume of black velvet worn with a gold-fringed waistcoat
and sticking by way of cravat a bunch of Parma violets in the opening of
a very low-necked shirt. Then he would invite parties of literary friends to

dinners that set all the world talking. In one instance in particular, modelling the entertainment on a banquet of the eighteenth century, he had organized a funeral feast in celebration of the most unmentionable of minor personal calamities. The dining-room was hung with black and looked out on a strangely metamorphosed garden, the walks being strewn with charcoal, the little basin in the middle of the lawn bordered with a rim of black basalt and filled with ink; and the ordinary shrubs superseded by cypresses and pines. The dinner itself was served on a black cloth, decorated with baskets of violets and scabiosae and illuminated by candelabra in which tall tapers flared.

While a concealed orchestra played funeral marches, the guests were waited on by naked negresses wearing shoes and stockings of cloth of silver besprinkled with tears.

The viands were served on black-bordered plates, – turtle soup, Russian black bread, ripe olives from Turkey, caviar, mule steaks, Frankfurt smoked sausages, game dished up in sauces coloured to resemble liquorice water and boot-blacking, truffles in jelly, chocolate-tinted creams, puddings, nectarines, fruit preserves, mulberries and cherries. The wines were drunk from dark-tinted glasses, – wines of the Limagne and Roussillon vintages, wines of Tenedos, the Val de Penas and Oporto. After the coffee and walnuts came other unusual beverages, kwas, porter and stout.

The invitations, which purported to be for a dinner in pious memory of the host's (temporarily) lost virility, were couched in the regulation phraseology of letters summoning relatives to attend the obsequies of a defunct kinsman.

But these extravagances, that had once been his boast, had died a natural death; nowadays his only feeling was one of self-contempt to remember these puerile and out-of-date displays of eccentricity, – the extraordinary clothes he had donned and the grotesque decorations he had lavished on his house. His only thought henceforth was to arrange, for his personal gratification only and no longer in order to startle other people, a home that should be comfortable, yet at the same time rich and rare in its appointments, to contrive himself a peaceful and exquisitely organized abode, specially adapted to meet the exigencies of the solitary life he proposed to lead.

Extract from *Studies in the History of the Renaissance* (1873)

WALTER PATER

The fount from which many a young aesthete drank, Walter Pater was slightly bemused by aestheticism, the movement he was accused of founding, but the influence of his Studies in the History of the Renaissance *on* Wilde et al. *was undeniable. This short extract from the conclusion argues passionately for individualism and intensity of living.*

Not the fruit of experience, but experience itself, is the end. A counted number of pulses only is given to us of a variegated, dramatic life. How may we see in them all that is to seen in them by the finest senses? How shall we pass most swiftly from point to point, and be present always at the focus where the greatest number of vital forces unite in their purest energy?

   To burn always with this hard, gem-like flame, to maintain this

ecstasy, is success in life. In a sense it might even be said that our failure is to form habits: for, after all, habit is relative to a stereotyped world, and meantime it is only the roughness of the eye that makes two persons, things, situations, seem alike. While all melts under our feet, we may well grasp at any exquisite passion, or any contribution to knowledge that seems by a lifted horizon to set the spirit free for a moment, or any stirring of the sense, strange dyes, strange colours, and curious odours, or work of the artist's hands, or the face of one's friend. Not to discriminate every moment some passionate attitude in those about us, and in the very brilliancy of their gifts some tragic dividing on their ways, is, on this short day of frost and sun, to sleep before evening. With this sense of the splendour of our experience and of its awful brevity, gathering all we are into one desperate effort to see and touch, we shall hardly have time to make theories about the things we see and touch. What we have to do is to be for ever curiously testing new opinions and courting new impressions, never acquiescing in a facile orthodoxy, of Comte, or of Hegel, or of our own. Philosophical theories or ideas, as points of view, instruments of criticism, may help us to gather up what might otherwise pass unregarded by us. 'Philosophy is the microscope of thought.' The theory or idea or system which requires of us the sacrifice of any part of this experience, in consideration of some interest into which we cannot enter, or some abstract theory we have not identified with ourselves, or of what is only conventional, has no real claim upon us.

'A First Sight of Verlaine' (1896)

EDMUND GOSSE

Here young English decadents bravely cross the Channel in search of their Parisian forebears: 'To race up and down the Boulevard St. Michel, catching live poets in shoals, what a charming game!'

In 1893 the thoughts of a certain pilgrim were a good deal occupied by the theories and experiments which a section of the younger French poets were engaged upon. In this country, the Symbolists and Decadents of Paris had been laughed at and parodied, but, with the exception of Mr. Arthur Symons, no English critic had given their tentatives any serious attention. I became much interested – not wholly converted, certainly, but considerably impressed – as I studied, not what was said about them by their enemies, but what they wrote themselves. Among them all, there was but one, Mallarmé, whom I knew personally; him I had met, more than twenty years before, carrying the vast folio of his Manet-Poe through the length and breadth of London, disappointed but not discouraged. I learned that there were certain haunts where these later Decadents might be observed in large numbers, drawn together by the gregarious attraction of verse. I determined to haunt that neighbourhood with a butterfly-net, and see what delicate creatures with powdery wings I could catch. And, above all, was it not understood that that vaster lepidopter, that giant hawk-moth, Paul Verlaine, uncoiled his proboscis in the same absinthe-corollas?

Timidity, doubtless, would have brought the scheme to nought, if, unfolding it to Henry Harland, who knows his Paris like the palm of his hand, he had not, with enthusiastic kindness, offered to become my cicerone. He was far from sharing my interest in the Symbolo-decadent movement, and the ideas of the 'poetes abscons comme la lune' left him a little cold yet he entered at once into the sport of the idea. To race up and down the Boulevard St. Michel, catching live poets in shoals, what a

charming game! So, with a beating heart and under this gallant guidance, I started on a beautiful April morning to try my luck as an entomologist. This is not the occasion to speak of the butterflies which we successfully captured during this and the following days and nights; the expedition was a great success. But, all the time, the hope of capturing that really substantial moth, Verlaine, was uppermost, and this is how it was realised.

As every one knows, the broad Boulevard St. Michel runs almost due south from the Palais de Justice to the Gardens of the Luxembourg. Through the greater part of its course, it is principally (so it strikes one) composed of restaurants and brasseries, rather dull in the daytime, excessively blazing and gay at night. To the critical entomologist the eastern side of this street is known as the chief, indeed almost the only habitat of *poeta symbolans*, which, however, occurs here in vast numbers. Each of the leaders of a school has his particular café, where he is to be found at an hour and in a chair known to the habitués of the place. So Dryden sat at Will's and Addison at Button's, when chocolate and ratafia, I suppose, took the place of absinthe. M. Jean Moréas sits in great circumstance at the Restaurant d'Harcourt — or he did three years ago — and there I enjoyed much surprising and stimulating conversation. But Verlaine — where was he? At his café, the François-Premier, we were told that he had not been seen for four days. 'There is a letter for him — he must be ill,' said Madame; and we felt what the tiger-hunter feels when the tiger has gone to visit a friend in another valley. But to persist is to succeed.

The last of three days devoted to this fascinating sport had arrived. I had seen Symbolists and Decadents to my heart's content. I had learned that Victor Hugo was not a poet at all, and that M. Gustave Kahn was a splendid bard; I had heard that neither Victor Hugo nor M. Gustave Kahn had a spark of talent, but that M. Charles Morice was the real Simon Pure. I had heard a great many conflicting opinions stated without hesitation and with a delightful violence; I had heard a great many verses recited which I did not understand because I was a foreigner, and could not have understood if I had been a Frenchman. I had quaffed a number of highly indigestible drinks, and had enjoyed myself very much. But I had not seen Verlaine, and poor Henry Harland was in despair. We invited some of the poets to dine with us that night (this is the etiquette of the 'Bou' Mich) at the Restaurant d'Harcourt, and a very entertaining meal we had. M. Moréas was in the chair, and a poetess with a charming name decorated us all with sprays of the *narcissus poeticus*. I suppose that the company was what is called 'a little mixed,' but I am sure it was very lyrical. I had the honour of giving my arm to a most amiable lady, the Queen of Golconda, whose precise rank among the crowned heads of Europe is, I am afraid, but vaguely determined. The dinner was simple, but distinctly good; the chairman was in magnificent form, un vrai chef d'école, and between each of the courses somebody intoned his own verses at the top of his voice. The windows were wide open on to the Boulevard, but there was no public expression of surprise.

It was all excessively amusing, but deep down in my consciousness, tolling like a little bell, there continued to sound the words, 'We haven't seen Verlaine.' I confessed as much at last to the sovereign of Golconda, and she was graciously pleased to say that she would make a great effort. She was kind enough, I believe, to send out a sort of search-party. Meanwhile, we adjourned to another café, to drink other things, and our company grew like a rolling snowball. I was losing all hope, and we were descending the Boulevard, our faces set for home; the Queen of Golconda was hanging heavily on my arm, and having formed a flattering misconception as to my age, was warning me against the temptations of Paris, when two more poets, a male and a female, most amiably hurried to meet us with the intoxicating news that Verlaine had been seen to dart into a little place called the Café Soleil d'Or. Thither we accordingly hied, buoyed up by hope, and our party, now comprising a dozen persons (all poets), rushed into an almost empty drinking-shop. But no Verlaine was to be seen. Moréas then collected us round a table, and fresh grenadines were ordered.

Where I sat, by the elbow of Moréas, I was opposite an open door, absolutely dark, leading down, by oblique stairs, to a cellar. As I idly watched this square of blackness I suddenly saw some ghostly shape fluttering at the bottom of it. It took the form of a strange bald head, bobbing close to the ground. Although it was so dim and vague, an idea crossed my mind. Not daring to speak, I touched Moréas, and so drew his attention to it. 'Pas un mot, pas un geste. Monsieur!' he whispered, and then, instructed in the guile of his race, insidias Danaum, the eminent author of *Les Cantilènes* rose, making a vague detour towards the street, and then plunged at the cellar door. There was a prolonged scuffle and a rolling downstairs; then Moréas reappeared triumphant; behind him something flopped up out of the darkness like an owl, – a timid shambling figure in a soft black hat, with jerking hands, and it peeped with intention to disappear again. But there were cries of 'Venez donc, Maître,' and by-and-by Verlaine was persuaded to emerge definitely and to sit by me.

I had been prepared for strange eccentricities of garb, but he was very decently dressed; he referred at once to the fact, and explained that this was the suit which had been bought for him to lecture in, in Belgium. He was particularly proud of a real white shirt; 'C'est ma chemise de conférence,' he said, and shot out the cuffs of it with pardonable pride. He was full of his experiences of Belgium, and in particular he said some very pretty things about Bruges and its beguinages, and how much he should like to spend the rest of his life there. Yet it seemed less the mediaeval buildings which had attracted him than a museum of old lace. He spoke with a veiled utterance, difficult for me to follow. Not for an instant would he take off his hat, so that I could not see the Socratic dome of forehead which figures in all the caricatures. I thought his countenance very Chinese, and I may perhaps say here that when he was in London in 1894 I called him a Chinese philosopher. He replied: 'Chinois – comme vous voulez, mais philosophe – non pas!'

On this first occasion (April 2, 1893), recitations were called for, and Verlaine repeated his Clair de Lune : –

'Votre âme est un paysage choisi
Que vont charmant masques et bergamasques
Jouant du luth et dansant et quasi
Tristes sous leurs déguisements fantasques,'

and presently, with a strange indifference to all incongruities of scene and company, part of his wonderful Mon Dieu m'a dit: –

'J'ai répondu: "Seigneur, vous avez dit mon âme.
C'est vrai que je vous cherche et ne vous trouve pas.
Mais vous aimer! Voyez comme je suis en bas,
Vous dont l'amour toujours monte comme la flamme

'Vous, la source de paix que toute soif réclame,
Helas! Voyez un peu tous mes tristes combats!
Oserai-je adorer la trace de vos pas,
Sur ces genoux saignants d'un rampement infame?"'

He recited in a low voice, without gesticulation, very delicately. Then M. Moréas, in exactly the opposite manner, with roarings of a bull and with modulated sawings of the air with his hand, intoned an eclogue addressed by himself to Verlaine as 'Tityre.' And so the exciting evening closed, the passionate shepherd in question presently disappearing again down those mysterious stairs. And we, out into the soft April night and the budding smell of the trees.

2

Art For Art's Sake – ARTIFICE

*The ego-mania of decadentism, its love of the artificial,
its aversion to nature, and to all forms of activity and
movement, its megalomaniacal contempt for men and its
exaggeration of the importance of art, have found their
English representative among the 'Æsthetes'.*
Max Nordau, *Degeneration*

Extracts from *Degeneration* (1892)

MAX NORDAU

A blistering jeremiad against all things decadent, this is an impassioned plea to reject all exponents of the moral degeneration haunting Europe. It's also a highly amusing jaunt through the psyche of the easily offended. As one often learns more of an argument by considering the counterpoints, I consider these extracts to be among the most important in this anthology. The hyperbolic outrage is delicious.

Decadentism has not been confined to France alone; it has also established a school in England. We have already mentioned, in the preceding book, one of the earliest and most servile imitators of Baudelaire – Swinburne. I had to class him among the mystics, for the degenerative stigma of mysticism predominates in all his works. He has, it is true, been train-bearer to so many models that he may be ranked among the domestic servants of a great number of masters; but, finally, he will be assigned a place where he has served longest, and that is among the pre-Raphaelites. From Baudelaire he has borrowed principally diabolism and Sadism, unnatural depravity, and a predilection for suffering, disease and crime. The ego-mania of decadentism, its love of the artificial, its aversion to nature, and to all forms of activity and movement, its megalomaniacal contempt for men and its exaggeration of the importance of art, have found their English representative among the 'Æsthetes,' the chief of whom is Oscar Wilde.

Wilde has done more by his personal eccentricities than by his works. Like Barbey d'Aurevilly, whose rose-coloured silk hats and gold lace cravats are well known, and like his disciple Joséphin Péladan, who walks about in lace frills and satin doublet, Wilde dresses in queer costumes which recall partly the fashions of the Middle Ages, partly the rococo modes. He pretends to have abandoned the dress of the present time because it offends his sense of the beautiful; but this is only a pretext in which probably he

himself does not believe. What really determines his actions is the hysterical craving to be noticed, to occupy the attention of the world with himself, to get talked about. It is asserted that he has walked down Pall Mall in the afternoon dressed in doublet and breeches, with a picturesque biretta on his head, and a sunflower in his hand, the quasi-heraldic symbol of the Æsthetes. This anecdote has been reproduced in all the biographies of Wilde, and I have nowhere seen it denied. But is a promenade with a sunflower in the hand also inspired by a craving for the beautiful?

Phasemakers are perpetually repeating the twaddle, that it is a proof of honourable independence to follow one's own taste without being bound down to the regulation costume of the Philistine cattle, and to choose for clothes the colours, materials and cut which appear beautiful to one's self, no matter how much they may differ from the fashion of the day. The answer to this cackle should be that it is above all a sign of anti-social ego-mania to irritate the majority unnecessarily, only to gratify vanity, or an æsthetical instinct of small importance and easy to control – such as is always done when, either by word or deed, a man places himself in opposition to this majority. He is obliged to repress many manifestations of opinions and desires out of regard for his fellow-creatures; to make him understand this is the aim of education, and he who has not learnt to impose some restraint upon himself in order not to shock others is called by malicious Philistines, not an Æsthete, but a blackguard.

The predilection for strange costume is a pathological aberration of a racial instinct. The adornment of the exterior has its origin in the strong desire to be admired by others – primarily by the opposite sex – to be recognised by them as especially well-shaped, handsome, youthful, or rich and powerful, or as preeminent through rank or merit. It is practised, then, with the object of producing a favourable impression on others, and is a result of thought about others, of preoccupation with the race. If, now, this

adornment be, not through mis-judgment but purposely, of a character to cause irritation to others, or lend itself to ridicule — in other words, if it excites disapproval instead of approbation — it then runs exactly counter to the object of the art of dress, and evinces a perversion of the instinct of vanity.

The pretence of a sense of beauty is the excuse of consciousness for a crank of the conscious. The fool who masquerades in Pall Mall does not see himself, and, therefore, does not enjoy the beautiful appearance which is supposed to be an æsthetic necessity for him. There would be some sense in his conduct if it had for its object an endeavour to cause others to dress in accordance with his taste; for them he sees, and they can scandalise him by the ugliness, and charm him by the beauty, of their costume. But to take the initiative in a new artistic style in dress brings the innovator not one hair's breadth nearer his assumed goal of æsthetic satisfaction.

When, therefore, an Oscar Wilde goes about in 'æsthetic costume' among gazing Philistines, exciting either their ridicule or their wrath, it is no indication of independence of character, but rather from a purely anti-socialistic, ego-maniacal recklessness and hysterical longing to make a sensation, justified by no exalted aim; nor is it from a strong desire for beauty, but from a malevolent mania for contradiction.

Be that as it may, Wilde obtained, by his buffoon mummery, a notoriety in the whole Anglo-Saxon world that his poems and dramas would never have acquired for him. I have no reason to trouble myself about these, since they are feeble imitations of Rossetti and Swinburne, and of dreary inanity. His prose essays, on the contrary, deserve attention, because they exhibit all the features which enable us to recognise in the 'Æsthete' the comrade in art of the Decadent.

Like his French masters, Oscar Wilde despises Nature. 'Whatever actually occurs is spoiled for art. All bad poetry springs from genuine feeling. To be natural is to be obvious, and to be obvious is to be inartistic.'

He is a 'cultivator of the Ego,' and feels deliciously indignant at the fact that Nature dares to be indifferent to his important person. 'Nature is so indifferent, so unappreciative. Whenever I am walking in the park here, I always feel that I am no more to her than the cattle that browse on the slope'.

With regard to himself and the human species, he shares the opinion of Des Esseintes. 'Ah! don't say that you agree with me. When people agree with me I always feel that I must be wrong'.

Oscar Wilde apparently admires immorality, sin and crime. In a very affectionate biographical treatise on Thomas Griffith Wainwright, designer, painter, and author, and the murderer of several people, he says: 'He was a forger of no mean or ordinary capabilities, and as a subtle and secret poisoner almost without rival in this or any age. This remarkable man, so powerful with "pen, pencil, and poison," etc. 'He sought to find expression by pen or poison'. 'When a friend reproached him with the murder of Helen Abercrombie, he shrugged his shoulders and said, 'Yes; it was a dreadful thing to do, but she had very thick ankles'. 'His crimes seem to have had an important effect upon his art. They gave a strong personality to his style, a quality that his early work certainly lacked'. 'There is no sin except stupidity'. 'An idea that is not dangerous is unworthy of being called an idea at all'.

He cultivates incidentally a slight mysticism in colours. 'He,' Wainwright, 'had that curious love of green which in individuals is always the sign of a subtle, artistic temperament, and in nations is said to denote a laxity, if not a decadence of morals'.

But the central idea of his tortuously disdainful prattling, pursuing as its chief aim the heckling of the Philistine, and laboriously seeking the opposite pole to sound common-sense, is the glorification of art.

Thus the doctrine of the 'Æsthetes' affirms, with the Parnassians, that the work of art is its own aim; with the Diabolists, that it need not be moral

– nay, were better to be immoral; with the Decadents, that it is to avoid, and be diametrically opposed to, the natural and the true; and with all these schools of the ego-mania of degeneration, that art is the highest of all human functions.

It is easily conceivable that the emotion expressed by the artist in his work may proceed from a morbid aberration, may be directed, in an unnatural, sensual, cruel manner, to what is ugly or loathsome. Ought we not in this case to condemn the work and, if possible, to suppress it? How can its right to exist be justified? By claiming that the artist was sincere when he created it, that he gave back what was really existing in him, and for that reason was subjectively justified in his artistic expansion? But there is a candour which is wholly inadmissible. The dipsomaniac and clastomaniac are sincere when they respectively drink or break everything within reach. We do not, however, acknowledge their right to satisfy their desire. We prevent them by force. We put them under guardianship, although their drunkenness and destructiveness may perhaps be injurious to no one but themselves. And still more decidedly does society oppose itself to the satisfaction of those cravings which cannot be appeased without violently acting upon others. The new science of criminal anthropology admits without dispute that homicidal maniacs, certain incendiaries, many thieves and vagabonds, act under an impulse; that through their crimes they satisfy an organic craving; that they outrage, kill, burn, idle, as others sit down to dinner, simply because they hunger to do so; but in spite of this and because of this, it demands that the appeasing of the sincere longings of these degenerate creatures be prevented by all means, and, if needs be, by their complete suppression. It never occurs to us to permit the criminal by organic disposition to 'expand' his individuality in crime, and just as little can it be expected of us to permit the degenerate artist to expand his individuality in immoral works of art. The artist who complacently represents what is reprehensible, vicious, criminal, approves of it, perhaps glorifies it, differs not in kind, but only in degree, from the criminal who actually commits it. It is a question of the intensity of the impulsion and the resisting power of the judgment, perhaps also of courage and cowardice; nothing else. If the actual law does not treat the criminal by intention so rigorously as the criminal in act, it is because criminal law pursues the deed, and not the purpose; the objective phenomenon, not its subjective roots. The Middle Ages had places of sanctuary where criminals could not be molested for their misdemeanours. Modern law has done away with this institution. Ought art to be at present the last asylum to which criminals may fly to escape punishment? Are they to be able to satisfy, in the so-called 'temple' of art, instincts which the policeman prevents them from appeasing in the street? I do not see how a privilege so inimical to society can be willingly defended.

I am far from sharing Ruskin's opinion that morality alone, and nothing else, can be demanded of a work of art. Morality alone is not sufficient. Otherwise religious tracts would be the finest literature, and the well-known coloured casts of sacred subjects turned out wholesale in Munich factories would be the choicest sculpture. Excellence of form maintains its rights in all the arts, and gives to the finest creation its artistic value. Hence the work need not be moral. More accurately, it need not be designed expressly to preach virtue and the fear of God, and to be destined for the edification of devotees. But between a work without sanctified aim and one of wilful immorality there is a world of difference. A work which is indifferent from a moral point of view will not be equally attractive or satisfying to all minds, but it will offend and repel no one. An explicitly immoral work excites in healthy persons the same feelings of displeasure and disgust as the immoral act itself, and the form of the work can change nothing of this. Most assuredly morality alone does not give beauty to a work of art. But beauty without morality is impossible.

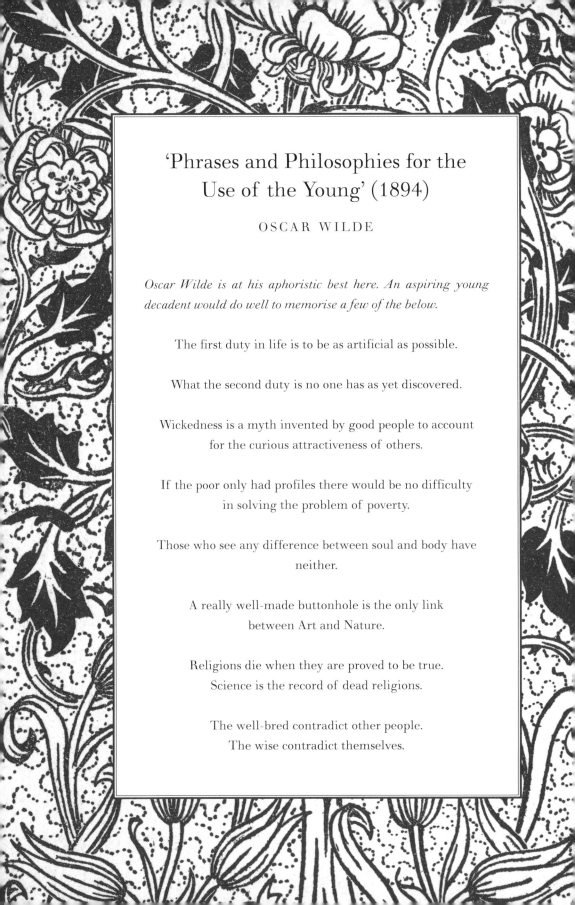

'Phrases and Philosophies for the Use of the Young' (1894)

OSCAR WILDE

Oscar Wilde is at his aphoristic best here. An aspiring young decadent would do well to memorise a few of the below.

The first duty in life is to be as artificial as possible.

What the second duty is no one has as yet discovered.

Wickedness is a myth invented by good people to account for the curious attractiveness of others.

If the poor only had profiles there would be no difficulty in solving the problem of poverty.

Those who see any difference between soul and body have neither.

A really well-made buttonhole is the only link between Art and Nature.

Religions die when they are proved to be true.
Science is the record of dead religions.

The well-bred contradict other people.
The wise contradict themselves.

Nothing that actually occurs is of the smallest importance.

Dullness is the coming of age of seriousness.

In all unimportant matters, style,
not sincerity is the essential.

In all important matters, style,
not sincerity is the essential.

If one tells the truth, one is sure,
sooner or later, to be found out.

Pleasure is the only thing one should live for.
Nothing ages like happiness.

It is only by not paying one's bills that one can hope
to live in the memory of the commercial classes.

No crime is vulgar, but all vulgarity is crime.
Vulgarity is the conduct of others.

Only the shallow know themselves.

Time is a waste of money.

One should always be a little improbable.

There is a fatality about all good resolutions.
They are invariably made too soon.

The only way to atone for being occasionally a little
overdressed is by being always absolutely over-educated.

To be premature is to be perfect.

Any preoccupation with ideas of what is right or wrong in
conduct shows an arrested intellectual development.

Ambition is the last refuge of the failure.

A truth ceases to be true when more than
one person believes in it.

In examinations the foolish ask questions
that the wise cannot answer.

Greek dress was in its essence inartistic.
Nothing should reveal the body but the body.

One should either be a work of art,
or wear a work of art.

It is only the superficial qualities that last.
Man's deeper nature is soon found out.

Industry is the root of all ugliness.

The ages live in history through their anachronisms.

It is only the gods who taste of death. Apollo has passed away,
but Hyacinth, whom men say he slew, lives on.

Nero and Narcissus are always with us.

The old believe everything: the middle-aged suspect
everything: the young know everything.

The condition of perfection is idleness:
the aim of perfection is youth.

Only the great masters of style ever succeed in being obscure.

There is something tragic about the enormous number
of young men there are in England at the present moment
who start life with perfect profiles, and end by
adopting some useful profession.

To love oneself is the beginning of a life-long romance.

Extracts from 'A Defence of Cosmetics' (1894)

MAX BEERBOHM

Published in the first edition of the Yellow Book, *'A Defence of Cosmetics'
caused something of a scandal. When the popular press got hold of it, they
vilified Beerbohm's wry celebration of make-up and artifice. His youthful
impudence is a joy to read in this ebullient and precocious piece.*

Nay, but it is useless to protest. Artifice must queen it once more in the
town, and so, if there be any whose hearts chafe at her return, let them not
say, 'We have come into evil times and be all for resistance, reformation, or
angry cavilling. For did the king's sceptre send the sea retrograde, or the
wand of the sorcerer avail to turn the sun from its old course? And what
man or what number of men ever stayed that inexorable process by which
the cities of this world grow, are very strong, fail, and grow again? Indeed,
indeed, there is charm in every period, and only fools and flutterpates do
not seek reverently for what is charming in their own day. No martyrdom,
however fine, nor satire, however splendidly bitter, has changed by a little
tittle the known tendency of things. It is the times that can perfect us, not
we the times, and so let all of us wisely acquiesce. Like the little wired
marionettes, let us acquiesce in the dance.

For behold! The Victorian era comes to its end and the day of sancta
simplicitas is quite ended. The old signs are here and the portents to warn
the seer of life that we are ripe for a new epoch of artifice. Are not men
rattling the dice-box and ladies dipping their fingers in the rouge-pot? At
Rome, in the keenest time of her *dégringolade*, when there was gambling
even in the holy temples, great ladies (does not Lucian tell us?) did not
scruple to squander all they had upon unguents from Arabia. Nero's
mistress and unhappy wife, Poppæa, of shameful memory, had in her
travelling retinue fifteen – or, as some say, fifty – she-asses, for the sake of
their milk, that was thought an incomparable guard against cosmetics
with poison in them. Last century, too, when life was lived by candle-light,

and ethics was but etiquette, and even art a question of punctilio, women, we know, gave the best hours of the day to the crafty farding of their faces and the towering of their coiffures. And men, throwing passion into the wine-bowl to sink or swim, turned out thought to browse upon the green cloth. Cannot we even now in our fancy see them, those silent exquisites round the long table at Brook's, masked, all of them, 'lest the countenance should betray feeling,' in quinze masks, through whose eyelets they sat peeping, peeping, while macao brought them riches or ruin! We can see them, those silent rascals, sitting there with their cards and their rouleaux and their wooden money-bowls long after the dawn had crept up St. James's and pressed its haggard face against the window of the little club. Yes, we can raise their ghosts – and, more, we can see anywhere a devotion to hazard fully as meek as theirs. In England there has been a wonderful revival of cards. Baccarat may rival dead faro in the tale of her devotees. We have all seen the sweet English chatelaine at her roulette wheel and ere long it may be that tender parents will be writing to complain of the compulsory baccarat in our public schools.

In fact, we are all gamblers once more, but our gambling is on a finer scale than ever it was. We fly from the card-room to the heath, and from the heath to the City, and from the City to the coast of the Mediterranean. And just as no one seriously encourages the clergy in its frantic efforts to lay the spirit of chance that has thus resurged among us, so no longer are many faces set against that other great sign of a more complicated life, the love for cosmetics. No longer is a lady of fashion blamed if, to escape the outrageous persecution of time, she fly for sanctuary to the toilet-table; and if a damsel, prying in her mirror, be sure that with brush and pigment she can trick herself into more charm, we are not angry. Indeed, why should we ever have been? Surely it is laudable, this wish to make fair the ugly and overtop fairness, and no wonder that within the last five years the trade of the makers of cosmetics has increased immoderately – twenty-fold, so one of these makers has said to me. We need but walk down any modish street and peer into the little broughams that flit past, or (in Thackeray's phrase) under the bonnet of any woman we meet, to see over how wide a kingdom rouge reigns.

And now that the use of pigments is becoming general, and most women are not so young as they are painted, it may be asked curiously how the prejudice ever came into being. Indeed, it is hard to trace folly, for that it is inconsequent, to its start; and perhaps it savours too much of reason to suggest that the prejudice was due to the tristful confusion man has made of soul and surface. Through trusting so keenly to the detection of the one by keeping watch upon the other, and by force of the thousand errors following, he has come to think of surface even as the reverse of soul. He seems to suppose that every clown beneath his paint and lipsalve is moribund and knows it (though in verity, I am told, clowns are as cheerful a class of men as any other), that the fairer the fruit's rind and the more delectable its bloom, the closer are packed the ashes within it. The very jargon of the hunting-field connects cunning with a mask. And so perhaps came man's anger at the embellishment of women – that lovely mask of enamel with its shadows of pink and tiny pencilled veins, what must lurk behind it? Of what treacherous mysteries may it not be the screen? Does not the heathen lacquer her dark face, and the harlot paint her cheeks, because sorrow has made them pale?

After all, the old prejudice is a-dying. We need not pry into the secret of its birth. Rather is this a time of jolliness and glad indulgence. For the era of rouge is upon us, and as only in an elaborate era can man, by the tangled accrescency of his own pleasures and emotions, reach that refinement which is his highest excellence, and by making himself, so to say, independent of Nature, come nearest to God, so only in an elaborate era is woman perfect. Artifice is the strength of the world, and in that same mask of paint and powder, shadowed with vermeil tint and most trimly pencilled, is woman's strength.

Loveliness shall sit at the toilet, watching her oval face in the oval mirror. Her smooth fingers shall flit among the paints and powder, to tip and mingle them, catch up a pencil, clasp a phial, and what not and what not, until the mask of vermeil tint has been laid aptly, the enamel quite hardened. And, heavens, how she will embarm us and ensorcel our eyes!

Positively rouge will rob us for a time of all our reason; we shall go mad over masks. Was it not at Capua that they had a whole street where nothing was sold but dyes and unguents? We must have such a street, and, to fill our new 'Seplasia'; our Arcade of the Unguents, all herbs and minerals and live creatures shall give of their substance. The white cliffs of Albion shall be ground to powder for Loveliness, and perfumed by the ghosts of many a little violet. The fluffy eider-ducks, that are swimming round the pond, shall lose their feathers, that the powder-puff may be moonlike as it passes over Loveliness' lovely face. Even the camels shall become ministers of delight, giving many tufts of their hair to be stained in her splendid colour-box. and across her cheek the swift hare's foot shall fly as of old. The sea shall offer her the phuchus, its scarlet weed. We shall spill the blood of mulberries at her bidding. And, as in another period of great ecstasy, a dancing wanton, le belle Aubrey, was crowned upon a church's lighted altar, so Arsenic, that 'greentress'd goddess,' ashamed at length of skulking between the soup of the unpopular and the test-tubes of the Queen's analyst, shall be exalted to a place of consummate honour upon the toilet-table of Loveliness.

All these things shall come to pass. Times of jolliness and glad indulgence! For Artifice, whom we drove forth, has returned among us, and, though her eyes are red with crying, she is smiling forgiveness. She is kind. Let us dance and be glad, and trip the cockawhoop! Artifice, sweetest exile, is come into her kingdom. Let us dance her a welcome!

'Maquillage' (1892)

ARTHUR SYMONS

A defence of cosmetics, in verse.

The charm of rouge on fragile cheeks,
    Pearl-powder, and, about the eyes,
The dark and lustrous eastern dyes;
    A voice of violets that speaks
Of perfumed hours of day, and doubtful night
Of alcoves curtained close against the light.

Gracile and creamy white and rose,
    Complexioned like the flower of dawn,
Her fleeting colours are as those
    That, from an April sky withdrawn,
Fade in a fragrant mist of tears away
When weeping noon leads on the altered day.

'Orchids' (1896)

THEODORE WRATISLAW

There was something pleasingly unnatural about the cultivation
of rare tropical plants in northern climes.

Orange and purple, shot with white and mauve,
Such in a greenhouse wet with tropic heat
One sees these delicate flowers whose parents throve
In some Pacific island's hot retreat.

Their ardent colours that betray the rank
Fierce hotbed of corruption whence they rose
Please eyes that long for stranger sweets than prank
Wild meadow-blooms and what the garden shows.

Exotic flowers! How great is my delight
To watch your petals curiously wrought,
To lie among your splendours day and night
Lost in a subtle dream of subtler thought.

Bathed in your clamorous orchestra of hues,
The palette of your perfumes, let me sleep
While your mesmeric presences diffuse
Weird dreams: and then bizarre sweet rhymes shall creep

Forth from my brain and slowly form and make
Sweet poems as a weaving spider spins,
A shrine of loves that laugh and swoon and ache,
A temple of coloured sorrows and perfumed sins.

'A Ballad of London' (1895)

RICHARD LE GALLIENNE

Richard Le Gallienne offers rhapsodic lines on London and modernity, while subtly positing it as the natural successor to Paris as the home of art and decadence.

AH, London! London! our delight,
Great flower that opens but at night,
Great City of the midnight sun,
Whose day begins when day is done.

Lamp after lamp against the sky
Opens a sudden beaming eye,
Leaping alight on either hand,
The iron lilies of the Strand.

Like dragonflies, the hansoms hover,
With jeweled eyes, to catch the lover;
The streets are full of lights and loves,
Soft gowns, and flutter of soiled doves.

The human moths about the light
Dash and cling close in dazed delight,
And burn and laugh, the world and wife,
For this is London, this is life!

Upon thy petals butterflies,
But at thy root, some say, there lies,
A world of weeping trodden things,
Poor worms that have not eyes or wings.

From out corruption of their woe
Springs this bright flower that charms us so,
Men die and rot deep out of sight
To keep this jungle-flower bright.

Paris and London, World-Flowers twain
Wherewith the World-Tree blooms again,
Since Time hath gathered Babylon,
And withered Rome still withers on.

Sidon and Tyre were such as ye,
How bright they shone upon the tree!
But Time hath gathered, both are gone,
And no man sails to Babylon.

Extract from *The Picture of Dorian Gray* (1891)

OSCAR WILDE

The Picture of Dorian Gray is a fabulous conflation of horror and beauty. The obsession with sense and sensation draws from Pater and Huysmans, but there is a unique Gothic grandeur at the heart of the tale. This extract delineates the pleasures to be found in the arcane pursuits of connoisseurship.

The worship of the senses has often, and with much justice, been decried, men feeling a natural instinct of terror about passions and sensations that seem stronger than themselves, and that they are conscious of sharing with the less highly organised forms of existence. But it appeared to Dorian Gray that the true nature of the senses had never been understood, and that they had remained savage and animal merely because the world had sought to starve them into submission or to kill them by pain, instead of aiming at making them elements of a new spirituality, of which a fine instinct for beauty was to be the dominant characteristic. As he looked back upon man moving through History, he was haunted by a feeling of loss. So much had been surrendered! and to such little purpose! There had been mad wilful rejections, monstrous forms of self-torture and self-denial, whose origin was fear, and whose result was a degradation infinitely more terrible than that fancied degradation from which, in their ignorance, they had sought to escape, Nature, in her wonderful irony, driving out the anchorite to feed with the wild animals of the desert and giving to the hermit the beasts of the field as his companions.

Yes: there was to be, as Lord Henry had prophesied, a new Hedonism that was to recreate life, and to save it from that harsh, uncomely puritanism that is having, in our own day, its curious revival. It was to have its service of the intellect, certainly; yet, it was never to accept any theory or system that would involve the sacrifice of any mode of passionate experience. Its aim, indeed, was to be experience itself, and not the fruits of experience, sweet or bitter as they might be. Of the asceticism that deadens the senses, as of the vulgar profligacy that dulls them, it was to know nothing. But it was to teach man to concentrate himself upon the moments of a life that is itself but a moment.

There are few of us who have not sometimes wakened before dawn, either after one of those dreamless nights that make us almost enamoured of death, or one of those nights of horror and misshapen joy, when through the chambers of the brain sweep phantoms more terrible than reality itself, and instinct with that vivid life that lurks in all grotesques, and that lends to Gothic art its enduring vitality, this art being, one might fancy, especially the art of those whose minds have been troubled with the malady of reverie. Gradually white fingers creep through the curtains, and they appear to tremble. In black fantastic shapes, dumb shadows crawl into the corners of the room, and crouch there. Outside, there is the stirring of birds among the leaves, or the sound of men going forth to their work, or the sigh and sob of the wind coming down from the hills, and wandering round the silent house, as though it feared to wake the sleepers, and yet must needs call forth sleep from her purple cave. Veil after veil of thin dusky gauze is lifted, and by degrees the forms and colours of things are restored to them, and we watch the dawn remaking the world in its antique pattern. The wan mirrors get back their mimic life. The flameless tapers stand where we had left them, and beside them lies the half-cut book that we had been studying, or the wired flower that we had worn at the ball, or the letter that we had been afraid to read, or that we had read too often. Nothing seems to us changed. Out of the unreal shadows of the night comes back the real life that we had known. We have to resume it where we had left off, and there steals over us a terrible sense of the necessity for the continuance of energy in the same wearisome round of stereotyped habits, or a wild longing, it may be, that our eyelids might open some morning upon a world that had been refashioned anew in the darkness for our pleasure, a world in which things would have fresh shapes and colours, and be changed, or have other secrets, a world in which the past would have little or no place, or survive, at any rate, in no conscious form of obligation or regret, the remembrance even of joy having its bitterness, and the memories of pleasure their pain.

It was the creation of such worlds as these that seemed to Dorian Gray to be the true object, or amongst the true objects, of life; and in his search for sensations that would be at once new and delightful, and possess that element of strangeness that is so essential to romance, he would often adopt certain modes of thought that he knew to be really alien to his nature, abandon himself to their subtle influences, and then, having, as it were, caught their colour and satisfied his intellectual curiosity, leave them with that curious indifference that is not incompatible with a real ardour of temperament, and that indeed, according to certain modern psychologists, is often a condition of it.

It was rumoured of him once that he was about to join the Roman Catholic communion; and certainly the Roman ritual had always a great attraction for him. The daily sacrifice, more awful really than all the sacrifices of the antique world, stirred him as much by its superb rejection of the evidence of the senses as by the primitive simplicity of its elements and the eternal pathos of the human tragedy that it sought to symbolise. He loved to kneel down on the cold marble pavement, and watch the priest, in his stiff flowered vestment, slowly and with white hands moving aside the veil of the tabernacle, or raising aloft the jewelled lantern-shaped monstrance with that pallid wafer that at times, one would fain think, is indeed the '*panis cælestis*,' the bread of angels, or, robed in the garments of the Passion of Christ, breaking the Host into the chalice, and smiting his breast for his sins. The fuming censers, that the grave boys, in their lace and scarlet, tossed into the air like great gilt flowers, had their subtle fascination for him. As he passed out, he used to look with wonder at the black confessionals, and long to sit in the dim shadow of one of them and listen to men and women whispering through the worn grating the true story of their lives.

But he never fell into the error of arresting his intellectual development by any formal acceptance of creed or system, or of mistaking, for a house in which to live, an inn that is but suitable for the sojourn of a night, or for a few hours of a night in which there are no stars and the moon is in travail. Mysticism, with its marvellous power of making common things strange to us, and the subtle antinomianism that always seems to accompany it, moved him for a season; and for a season he inclined to the materialistic doctrines of the *Darwinismus* movement in Germany, and found a curious pleasure in tracing the thoughts and passions of men to some pearly cell in the brain, or some white nerve in the body, delighting in the conception of the absolute dependence of the spirit on certain physical conditions, morbid or healthy, normal or diseased. Yet, as has been said of him before, no theory of life seemed to him to be of any importance compared with life itself. He felt keenly conscious of how barren all intellectual speculation is when separated from action and experiment. He knew that the senses, no less than the soul, have their spiritual mysteries to reveal.

And so he would now study perfumes, and the secrets of their manufacture, distilling heavily-scented oils, and burning odorous gums from the East. He saw that there was no mood of the mind that had not its counterpart in the sensuous life, and set himself to discover their true relations, wondering what there was in frankincense that made one mystical, and in ambergris that stirred one's passions, and in violets that woke the memory of dead romances, and in musk that troubled the brain, and in champak that stained the imagination; and seeking often to elaborate a real psychology of perfumes, and to estimate the several influences of sweet-smelling roots, and scented pollen-laden flowers, or aromatic balms, and of dark and fragrant woods, of spikenard that sickens, of hovenia that makes men mad, and of aloes that are said to be able to expel melancholy from the soul.

At another time he devoted himself entirely to music, and in a long latticed room, with a vermilion-and-gold ceiling and walls of olive-green lacquer, he used to give curious concerts, in which mad gypsies tore wild music from little zithers, or grave yellow-shawled Tunisians plucked at the strained strings of monstrous lutes, while grinning negroes beat monotonously upon copper drums, and, crouching upon scarlet mats, slim turbaned Indians blew through long pipes of reed or brass, and charmed, or feigned to charm, great hooded snakes and horrible horned adders. The harsh intervals and shrill discords of barbaric music stirred him at times when Schubert's grace, and Chopin's beautiful sorrows, and the mighty harmonies of Beethoven himself, fell unheeded on his ear. He collected together from all parts of the world the strangest instruments that could be found, either in the tombs of dead nations or among the few savage tribes that have survived contact with Western civilisations, and loved to touch and try them. He had the mysterious *juruparis* of the Rio Negro Indians, that women are not allowed to look at, and that even youths may not see till they have been subjected to fasting and scourging, and the earthen jars of the Peruvians that have the shrill cries of birds, and flutes of human bones such as Alfonso de Ovalle heard in Chile, and the sonorous green jaspers that are found near Cuzco and give forth a note of singular sweetness. He had painted gourds filled with pebbles that rattled when they were shaken; the long *clarin* of the Mexicans, into which the performer does not blow, but through which he inhales the air; the harsh *ture* of the Amazon tribes, that is sounded by the sentinels who sit all day long in high trees, and can be heard, it is said, at a distance of three leagues; the *teponaztli*, that has two vibrating tongues of wood, and is beaten with sticks that are smeared with an elastic gum obtained from the milky juice of plants; the *yotl*-bells of the Aztecs, that are hung in clusters like grapes; and a huge cylindrical drum, covered with the skins of great serpents, like the one that Bernal Diaz saw when he went with Cortes into the Mexican temple, and of whose doleful sound he has left us so vivid a description. The fantastic character of these instruments fascinated him, and he felt a curious delight in the thought that Art, like Nature, has her monsters, things of bestial shape and with hideous voices. Yet, after some time, he wearied of them, and would sit in his box at the opera, either alone or with Lord Henry, listening in rapt pleasure to 'Tannhäuser' and seeing in the prelude to that great work of art a presentation of the tragedy of his own soul.

On one occasion he took up the study of jewels, and appeared at a costume ball as Anne de Joyeuse, Admiral of France, in a dress covered with five hundred and sixty pearls. This taste enthralled him for years, and, indeed, may be said never to have left him. He would often spend a whole day settling and resettling in their cases the various stones that he had collected, such as the olive-green chrysoberyl that turns red by lamp-light, the cymophane with its wire-like line of silver, the pistachio-coloured peridot, rose-pink and wine-yellow topazes, carbuncles of fiery scarlet with tremulous four-rayed stars, flame-red cinnamon-stones, orange and violet spinels, and amethysts with their alternate layers of ruby and sapphire. He loved the red gold of the sunstone, and the moonstone's pearly whiteness, and the broken rainbow of the milky opal. He procured from Amsterdam three emeralds of extraordinary size and richness of colour, and had a turquoise *de la vieille roche* that was the envy of all the connoisseurs.

He discovered wonderful stories, also, about jewels. In Alphonso's 'Clericalis Disciplina' a serpent was mentioned with eyes of real jacinth, and in the romantic history of Alexander, the Conqueror of Emathia was said to have found in the vale of Jordan snakes 'with collars of real emeralds growing on their backs.' There was a gem in the brain of the dragon, Philostratus told us, and 'by the exhibition of golden letters and a scarlet robe' the monster could be thrown into a magical sleep, and slain. According to the great alchemist, Pierre de Boniface, the diamond rendered a man invisible, and the agate of India made him eloquent. The cornelian appeased anger, and the hyacinth provoked sleep, and the amethyst drove away the fumes of wine. The garnet cast out demons, and the hydropicus deprived the moon of her colour. The selenite waxed and waned with the moon, and the meloceus, that discovers thieves, could be affected only by the blood of kids. Leonardus Camillus had seen a white stone taken from the brain of a newly-killed toad, that was a certain antidote against poison. The bezoar, that was found in the heart of the Arabian deer, was a charm that could cure the plague. In the nests of Arabian birds was the aspilates, that, according to Democritus, kept the wearer from any danger by fire.

The King of Ceilan rode through his city with a large ruby in his hand, at the ceremony of his coronation. The gates of the palace of John the Priest were 'made of sardius, with the horn of the horned snake inwrought, so that no man might bring poison within.' Over the gable were 'two golden apples, in which were two carbuncles,' so that the gold might shine by day, and the

carbuncles by night. In Lodge's strange romance 'A Margarite of America'
it was stated that in the chamber of the queen one could behold 'all the
chaste ladies of the world, inchased out of silver, looking through fair
mirrours of chrysolites, carbuncles, sapphires, and greene emeraults.'
Marco Polo had seen the inhabitants of Zipangu place rose-coloured pearls
in the mouths of the dead. A sea-monster had been enamoured of the
pearl that the diver brought to King Perozes, and had slain the thief, and
mourned for seven moons over its loss. When the Huns lured the king into
the great pit, he flung it away — Procopius tells the story — nor was it ever

found again, though the Emperor Anastasius offered five hundred-weight of gold pieces for it. The King of Malabar had shown to a certain Venetian a rosary of three hundred and four pearls, one for every god that he worshipped.

When the Duke de Valentinois, son of Alexander VI, visited Louis XII of France, his horse was loaded with gold leaves, according to Brantôme, and his cap had double rows of rubies that threw out a great light. Charles of England had ridden in stirrups hung with four hundred and twenty-one diamonds. Richard II had a coat, valued at thirty thousand marks, which was covered with balas rubies. Hall described Henry VIII, on his way to the Tower previous to his coronation, as wearing 'a jacket of raised gold, the placard embroidered with diamonds and other rich stones, and a great bauderike about his neck of large balasses.' The favourites of James I wore earrings of emeralds set in gold filigrane. Edward II gave to Piers Gaveston a suit of red-gold armour studded with jacinths, a collar of gold roses set with turquoise-stones, and a skull-cap *parsemé* with pearls. Henry II wore jewelled gloves reaching to the elbow, and had a hawk-glove sewn with twelve rubies and fifty-two great orients. The ducal hat of Charles the Rash, the last Duke of Burgundy of his race, was hung with pear-shaped pearls, and studded with sapphires.

How exquisite life had once been! How gorgeous in its pomp and decoration! Even to read of the luxury of the dead was wonderful.

Then he turned his attention to embroideries, and to the tapestries that performed the office of frescoes in the chill rooms of the Northern nations of Europe. As he investigated the subject – and he always had an extraordinary faculty of becoming absolutely absorbed for the moment in whatever he took up – he was almost saddened by the reflection of the ruin that Time brought on beautiful and wonderful things. He, at any rate, had escaped that. Summer followed summer, and the yellow jonquils bloomed and died many times, and nights of horror repeated the story of their shame, but he was unchanged. No winter marred his face or stained his flower-like bloom. How different it was with material things! Where had they passed to? Where was the great crocus-coloured robe, on which the gods fought against the giants, that had been worked by brown girls for the pleasure of Athena? Where, the huge velarium that Nero had stretched across the Colosseum at Rome, that Titan sail of purple on which was represented the starry sky, and Apollo driving a chariot drawn by white gilt-reined steeds? He longed to see the curious table-napkins wrought for the Priest of the Sun, on which were displayed all the dainties and viands that could be wanted for a feast; the mortuary cloth of King Chilperic, with its three hundred golden bees; the fantastic robes that excited the indignation of the Bishop of Pontus, and were figured with 'lions, panthers, bears, dogs, forests, rocks, hunters – all, in fact, that a painter can copy from nature;' and the coat that Charles of Orleans once wore, on the sleeves of which were embroidered the verses of a song beginning 'Madame, je suis tout joyeux,' the musical accompaniment of the words being wrought in gold thread, and each note, of square shape in those days, formed with four pearls. He read of the room that was prepared at the palace at Rheims for the use of Queen Joan of Burgundy, and was decorated with 'thirteen hundred and twenty-one parrots, made in broidery, and blazoned with the king's arms, and five hundred and sixty-one butterflies, whose wings were similarly ornamented with the arms of the queen, the whole worked in gold.' Catherine de Médicis had a mourning-bed made for her of black velvet powdered with crescents and suns. Its curtains were of damask, with leafy wreaths and garlands, figured upon a gold and silver ground, and fringed along the edges with broideries of pearls, and it stood in a room hung with rows of the queen's devices in cut black velvet upon cloth of silver. Louis XIV had gold embroidered caryatides fifteen feet high in his apartment. The state bed of Sobieski, King of Poland, was made of Smyrna gold brocade embroidered in turquoises with verses from the Koran. Its supports were of silver gilt, beautifully chased, and profusely set with enamelled and jewelled medallions. It had been taken from the Turkish camp before Vienna, and the standard of Mohammed had stood beneath the tremulous gilt of its canopy.

And so, for a whole year, he sought to accumulate the most exquisite specimens that he could find of textile and embroidered work, getting the dainty Delhi muslins, finely wrought with gold-thread palmates, and stitched over with iridescent beetles' wings; the Dacca gauzes, that from their transparency are known in the East as 'woven air,' and 'running water,' and 'evening dew'; strange figured cloths from Java; elaborate yellow Chinese hangings; books bound in tawny satins or fair blue silks, and wrought with *fleurs de lys*, birds, and images; veils of *lacis* worked in Hungary point; Sicilian brocades, and stiff Spanish velvets; Georgian work with its gilt coins, and Japanese *Foukousas* with their green-toned golds and their marvellously-plumaged birds.

He had a special passion, also, for ecclesiastical vestments, as indeed he had for everything connected with the service of the Church. In the long cedar chests that lined the west gallery of his house he had stored away many rare and beautiful specimens of what is really the raiment of the Bride of Christ, who must wear purple and jewels and fine linen that she may hide the pallid macerated body that is worn by the suffering that she seeks for, and wounded by self-inflicted pain. He possessed a gorgeous cope of crimson silk and gold-thread damask, figured with a repeating pattern of golden pomegranates set in six-petalled formal blossoms, beyond which on either side was the pine-apple device wrought in seed-pearls. The orphreys were divided into panels representing scenes from the life of the Virgin, and the coronation of the Virgin was figured in coloured silks upon the hood. This was Italian work of the fifteenth century. Another cope was of green velvet, embroidered with heart-shaped groups of acanthus-leaves, from which spread long-stemmed white blossoms, the details of which were picked out with silver thread and coloured crystals. The morse bore a seraph's head in gold-thread raised work. The orphreys were woven in a diaper of red and gold silk, and were starred with medallions of many saints and martyrs, among whom was St. Sebastian. He had chasubles, also, of amber-coloured silk, and blue silk and gold brocade, and yellow silk damask and cloth of gold, figured with representations of the Passion and Crucifixion of Christ, and embroidered with lions and peacocks and other emblems; dalmatics of white satin and pink silk damask, decorated with tulips and dolphins and *fleurs de lys*; altar frontals of crimson velvet and blue linen; and many corporals, chalice-veils, and sudaria. In the mystic offices to which such things were put, there was something that quickened his imagination.

For these treasures, and everything that he collected in his lovely house, were to be to him means of forgetfulness, modes by which he could escape, for a season, from the fear that seemed to him at times to be almost too great to be borne. Upon the walls of the lonely locked room where he had spent so much of his boyhood, he had hung with his own hands the terrible portrait whose changing features showed him the real degradation of his life, and in front of it had draped the purple-and-gold pall as a curtain. For weeks he would not go there, would forget the hideous painted thing, and get back his light heart, his wonderful joyousness, his passionate absorption in mere existence. Then, suddenly, some night he would creep out of the house, go down to dreadful places near Blue Gate Fields, and stay there, day after day, until he was driven away. On his return he would sit in front of the picture, sometimes loathing it and himself, but filled, at other times, with that pride of individualism that is half the fascination of sin, and smiling with secret pleasure, at the misshapen shadow that had to bear the burden that should have been his own.

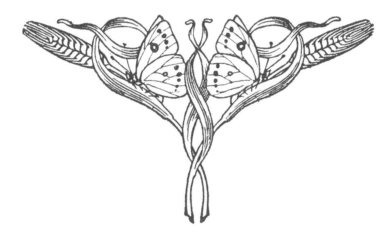

'Peacocks: A Mood' (1902)

OLIVE CUSTANCE

A subtle and beautiful poem from one of the major female writers of the movement. The bisexual Custance was the wife of Lord Alfred Douglas – Oscar Wilde's lover – and joined their mostly male literary circle. Peacocks, along with orchids, were a common motif of the era, used to encode beauty, eccentricity, art, divinity, individuality and sexuality. The poem evokes a homoerotic Eden destined to fall.

In gorgeous plumage, azure, gold and green,
They trample the pale flowers, and their shrill cry
Troubles the garden's bright tranquillity!
Proud birds of Beauty, splendid and serene,
Spreading their brilliant fans, screen after screen
Of burnished sapphire, gemmed with mimic suns –
Strange magic eyes that, so the legend runs,
Will bring misfortune to this fair demesne...

And my gay youth, that, vain and debonair,
Sits in the sunshine – tired at last of play
(A child, that finds the morning all too long),
Tempts with its beauty that disastrous day
When in the gathering darkness of despair
Death shall strike dumb the laughing mouth of song.

'The Décadent to His Soul' (1892)

RICHARD LE GALLIENNE

*The pointed (and pointless) spelling of décadent takes a swipe at
the excesses of decadence and the movement's Francophilia. Yet
the Liverpudlian poet added a 'Le' to his own name.*

The Décadent was speaking to his soul –
Poor useless thing, he said,
Why did God burden me with such as thou?
The body were enough,
The body gives me all.

The soul's a sort of sentimental wife
That prays and whimpers of the higher life,
Objects to latch-keys, and bewails the old,
The dear old days, of passion and of dream,
When life was a blank canvas, yet untouched
Of the great painter Sin.

Yet, little soul, thou hast fine eyes,
And knowest fine airy motions,
Hast a voice –
Why wilt thou so devote them to the church?

His face grew strangely sweet –
As when a toad smiles.
He dreamed of a new sin:
An incest 'twixt the body and the soul.

He drugged his soul, and in a house of sin
She played all she remembered out of heaven
For him to kiss and clip by.
He took a little harlot in his hands,
And she made all his veins like boiling oil,
Then that grave organ made them cool again.

Then from that day, he used his soul
As bitters to the over dulcet sins,
As olives to the fatness of the feast —
She made those dear heart-breaking ecstasies
Of minor chords amid the Phrygian flutes,
She sauced his sins with splendid memories,
Starry regrets and infinite hopes and fears;
His holy youth and his first love
Made pearly background to strange-coloured vice.

Sin is no sin when virtue is forgot.
It is so good in sin to keep in sight
The white hills whence we fell, to measure by —
To say I was so high, so white, so pure,
And am so low, so blood-stained and so base;
I revel here amid the sweet sweet mire
And yonder are the hills of morning flowers;
So high, so low; so lost and with me yet;
To stretch the octave 'twixt the dream and deed,
Ah, that's the thrill!
To dream so well, to do so ill, —
There comes the bitter-sweet that makes the sin.

First drink the stars, then grunt amid the mire,
So shall the mire have something of the stars,
And the high stars be fragrant of the mire.

The Décadent was speaking to his soul –
Dear witch, I said the body was enough.
How young, how simple as a suckling child!
And then I dreamed – 'an incest 'twixt the body and the soul:'
Let's wed, I thought, the seraph with the dog,
And wait the purple thing that shall be born.

And now look round – seest thou this bloom?
Seven petals and each petal seven dyes,
The stem is gilded and the root in blood:
That came of thee.
Yea, all my flowers were single save for thee.
I pluck seven fruits from off a single tree,
I pluck seven flowers from off a single stem,
I light my palace with the seven stars,
And eat strange dishes to Gregorian chants:
All thanks to thee.

But the soul wept with hollow hectic face,
Captive in that lupanar of a man.

And I who passed by heard and wept for both –
The man was once an apple-cheek dear lad,
The soul was once an angel up in heaven.

O let the body be a healthy beast,
And keep the soul a singing soaring bird;
But lure thou not the soul from out the sky
To pipe unto the body in the sty.

'The Cultured Fawn' (1891)

LIONEL JOHNSON

A beautifully acerbic take-down of the decadents, written by a fringe member of the group. The essay was published anonymously in the Anti-Jacobin.

He, or shall we say it? is a curious creature; tedious after a time, when you have got its habits by heart, but certainly curious on first acquaintance. You breed it in this way:

Take a young man, who had brains as a boy, and teach him to disbelieve everything that his elders believe in matters of thought, and to reject everything that seems true to himself in matters of sentiment. He need not be at all revolutionary; most clever youths for mere experience's sake will discard their natural or acquired convictions. He will then, since he is intelligent and bright, want something to replace his early notions. If Aristotle's *Poetics* are absurd, and Pope is no poet, and politics are vulgar, and Carlyle is played out, and Mr. Ruskin is tiresome, and so forth, according to the circumstances of the case, our youth will be bored to death by the nothingness of everything. You must supply him with the choicest delicacies, and feed him upon the finest rarities. And what so choice as a graceful affectation, or so fine as a surprising paradox? So you cast about for these two, and at once you see that many excellent affectations and paradoxes have had their day. A treasured melancholy of the German moonlight sort, a rapt enthusiasm in the Byronic style, a romantic eccentricity after the French fashion of 1830, a 'frank, fierce,' sensuousness *à la jeunesse Swinburnienne*, our youth might flourish them in the face of society all at once, without receiving a single invitation to private views or suppers of the elect. And, in truth, it requires a positive genius for the absurd to discover a really promising affectation, a thoroughly fascinating paradox. But the last ten years have done it. And a remarkable achievement it is.

Externally, our hero should cultivate a reassuring sobriety of habit, with just a dash of the dandy. None of the wandering looks, the elaborate

disorder, the sublime lunacy of his predecessor, the 'apostle of culture.'
Externally, then, a precise appearance; internally, a catholic sympathy with
all that exists, and 'therefore' suffers, for art's sake. Now art, at present, is
not a question of the senses so much as of the nerves. Botticelli, indeed,
was very precious, but Baudelaire is very nervous. Gautier was adorably
sensuous, but M. Verlaine is pathetically sensitive. That is the point:
exquisite appreciation of pain, exquisite thrills of anguish, exquisite
adoration of suffering. Here comes in a tender patronage of Catholicism:
white tapers upon the high altar, an ascetic and beautiful young priest, the
great gilt monstrance, the subtle-scented and mystical incense, the old
world accents of the Vulgate, of the Holy Offices; the splendour of the
sacred vestments. We kneel at some hour, not too early for our convenience,
repeating that solemn Latin, drinking in those Gregorian tones, with
plenty of modern French sonnets in memory, should the sermon be dull.
But to join the Church! Ah, no! better to dally with the enchanting
mysteries, to pass from our dreams of delirium to our dreams of sanctity
with no coarse facts to jar upon us. And so these refined persons cherish a
double 'passion,' the sentiment of repentant yearning and the sentiment of
rebellious sin.

To play the part properly a flavor of cynicism is recommended: a
scientific profession of materialist dogmas, coupled — for you should
forswear consistency — with gloomy chatter about 'The Will to Live.' If you
can say it in German, so much the better; a gross tongue, partially redeemed
by Heine, but an infallible oracle of scepticism. Jumble all these
'impressions' together, your sympathies and your sorrows, your devotion
and your despair; carry them about with you in a State of fermentation,
and finally conclude that life is loathsome yet that beauty is beatific. And
beauty — ah, beauty is everything beautiful! Isn't that a trifle obvious, you
say? That is the charm of it, it shows your perfect simplicity, your chaste
and catholic innocence. Innocence of course: beauty is always innocent,
ultimately. No doubt there are 'monstrous' things, terrible pains, the
haggard eyes of an *absintheur*, the pallid faces of 'neurotic' sinners; but all
that is the portion of our Parisian friends, such and such a 'group of artists,'
who meet at the Café So-and-So. We like people to think we are much the

same, but it isn't true. We are quite harmless, we only concoct strange and subtle verse about it. And, anyway, beauty includes everything; there's another sweet saying for you from our 'impressionist' copy-books. Impressions! that is all. Life is mean and vulgar, Members of Parliament are odious, the critics are commercial pedants: we alone know Beauty, and Art, and Sorrow, and Sin. Impressions! exquisite, dainty fantasies; fiery-colored visions; and impertinence straggling into epigram, for 'the true' criticism; *c'est adorable*! And since we are scholars and none of your penny-a-line Bohemians, we throw in occasional doses of 'Hellenism': by which we mean the Ideal of the Cultured Faun. That is to say, a flowery Paganism, such as no 'Pagan' ever had; a mixture of 'beautiful woodland natures,' and 'the perfect comeliness of the Parthenon frieze,' together with the elegant languors and favourite vices of (let us parade our 'decadent' learning) the *Stratonis Epigrammata*. At this time of day we need not dilate upon the equivocal charm of everything Lesbian. And who shall assail us? – what stupid and uncultured critic, what coarse and narrow Philistine? We are the Elect of Beauty: saints and sinners, devils and devotees, Athenians and Parisians, Romans of the Empire and Italians of the Renaissance. *Fin de siécle! fin de siécle!* Literature is a thing of beauty, blood, and nerves.

Let the Philistine critic have the last word; let him choose his words with all care, and define in his rough fashion. How would it do to call the Cultured Faun a feeble and a foolish beast?

3

Madder Music, Stronger Wine! —INTOXICATION

Whiskey and beer for fools; absinthe for poets; absinthe has the power of the magicians; it can wipe out or renew the past, and annul or foretell the future.
Ernest Dowson

Extracts from 'Absinthe:
The Green Goddess' (1918)

ALEISTER CROWLEY

Absinthe is more of a concept than a drink because the exact recipe has always varied enormously – angelica, calamus, coriander, dittany, hyssop, liquorice, marjoram, melissa, mugwort, nutmeg, oregano, sweet flag and star anise have all been used as admixtures besides the essential wormwood, fennel and aniseed. Absinthe is as much a magic potion as it is a liqueur. It is therefore fitting that one the best texts written about absinthe is this one by the notorious Aleister Crowley, in which he declares, 'Ah! The Green Goddess! What is the fascination that makes her so adorable and so terrible?'

I

Keep always this dim corner for me, that I may sit while the Green Hour glides, a proud pavine of Time. For I am no longer in the city accursed, where Time is horsed on the white gelding Death, his spurs rusted with blood.

There is a corner of the United States which he has overlooked. It lies in New Orleans, between Canal Street and Esplanade Avenue; the Mississippi for its base. Thence it reaches northward to a most curious desert land, where is a cemetery lovely beyond dreams. Its walls low and whitewashed, within which straggles a wilderness of strange and fantastic tombs; and hard by is that great city of brothels which is so cynically mirthful a neighbor. As Felicien Rops wrote, – or was it Edmond d'Haraucourt? – *'la Prostitution et la Mort sont frère et soeur – les fils de Dieu!'* At least the poet of *Le Legende des Sexes* was right, and the psycho-analysts after him, in identifying the Mother with the Tomb. This, then, is only the beginning and end of things, this *'quartier macabre'* beyond the North Rampart with the Mississippi on the other side. It is like the space between, our life which flows, and fertilizes as it flows, muddy and malarious as it may be, to empty itself into the warm bosom of the Gulf

Stream, which (in our allegory) we may call the Life of God.

But our business is with the heart of things; we must go beyond the crude phenomena of nature if we are to dwell in the spirit. Art is the soul of life and the Old Absinthe House is heart and soul of the old quarter of New Orleans.

For here was the headquarters of no common man — no less than a real pirate — of Captain Lafitte, who not only robbed his neighbors, but defended them against invasion. Here, too, sat Henry Clay, who lived and died to give his name to a cigar. Outside this house no man remembers much more of him than that; but here, authentic and, as I imagine, indignant, his ghost stalks grimly.

Here, too are marble basins hollowed — and hallowed! — by the drippings of the water which creates by baptism the new spirit of absinthe.

I am only sipping the second glass of that 'fascinating, but subtle poison, whose ravages eat men's heart and brain' that I have ever tasted in my life; and as I am not an American anxious for quick action, I am not surprised and disappointed that I do not drop dead upon the spot. But I can taste souls without the aid of absinthe; and besides, this is magic of absinthe! The spirit of the house has entered into it; it is an elixir, the masterpiece of an old alchemist, no common wine.

And so, as I talk with the patron concerning the vanity of things, I perceive the secret of the heart of God himself; this, that everything, even the vilest thing, is so unutterably lovely that it is worthy of the devotion of a God for all eternity.

What other excuse could He give man for making him? In substance, that is my answer to King Solomon.

II

The barrier between divine and human things is frail but inviolable; the artist and the bourgeois are only divided by a point of view — 'A hair divided the false and true.'

I am watching the opalescence of my absinthe, and it leads me to ponder upon a certain very curious mystery, persistent in legend. We may call it the mystery of the rainbow.

Originally in the fantastic but significant legend of the Hebrews, the rainbow is mentioned as the sign of salvation. The world has been purified by water, and was ready for the revelation of Wine. God would never again destroy His work, but ultimately seal its perfection by a baptism of fire.

Now, in this analogue also falls the coat of many colors which was made for Joseph, a legend which was regarded as so important that it was subsequently borrowed for the romance of Jesus. The veil of the Temple, too, was of many colors. We find, further east, that the *Manipura Cakkra* – the Lotus of the City of Jewels – which is an important centre in Hindu anatomy, and apparently identical with the solar plexus, is the central point of the nervous system of the human body, dividing the sacred from the profane, or the lower from the higher.

In western Mysticism, once more we learn that the middle grade initiation is called *Hodos Camelioniis*, the Path of the Chameleon. There is here evidently an illusion to this same mystery. We also learn that the middle stage in Alchemy is when the liquor becomes opalescent.

Finally, we note among the visions of the Saints one called the Universal Peacock, in which the totality is perceived thus royally appareled.

Would it were possible to assemble in this place the cohorts of quotation; for indeed they are beautiful with banners, flashing their myriad rays from cothurn and habergeon, gay and gallant in the light of that Sun which knows no fall from Zenith of high noon!

Yet I must needs already have written so much to make clear one pitiful conceit: can it be that in the opalescence of absinthe is some occult link with this mystery of the Rainbow? For undoubtedly one does indefinably and subtly insinuate the drinker in the secret chamber of Beauty, does kindle his thoughts to rapture, adjust his point of view to that of the artists, at least to that degree of which he is originally capable, weave for his fancy a gala dress of stuff as many-colored as the mind of Aphrodite.

Oh Beauty! Long did I love thee, long did I pursue thee, thee elusive, thee intangible! And lo! thou enfoldest me by night and day in the arms of gracious, of luxurious, of shimmering silence.

III

The Prohibitionist must always be a person of no moral character; for he cannot even conceive of the possibility of a man capable of resisting temptation. Still more, he is so obsessed, like the savage, by the fear of the unknown, that he regards alcohol as a fetish, necessarily alluring and tyrannical.

With this ignorance of human nature goes an ever grosser ignorance of the divine nature. He does not understand that the universe has only one possible purpose; that, the business of life being happily completed by the production of the necessities and luxuries incidental to comfort, the residuum of human energy needs an outlet. The surplus of Will must find issue in the elevation of the individual towards the Godhead; and the method of such elevation is by religion, love, and art. These three things are indissolubly bound up with wine, for they are species of intoxication.

Yet against all these things we find the prohibitionist, logically enough. It is true that he usually pretends to admit religion as a proper pursuit for humanity; but what a religion! He has removed from it every element of ecstasy or even of devotion; in his hands it has become cold, fanatical, cruel, and stupid, a thing merciless and formal, without sympathy or humanity. Love and art he rejects altogether; for him the only meaning of love is a mechanical – hardly even physiological! – process necessary for the perpetuation of the human race. (But why perpetuate it?) Art is for him the parasite and pimp of love. He cannot distinguish between the Apollo Belvedere and the crude bestialities of certain Pompeian frescoes, or between Rabelais and Elinor Glyn.

What then is his ideal of human life? one cannot say. So crass a creature can have no true ideal. There have been ascetic philosophers; but the prohibitionist would be as offended by their doctrine as by ours, which, indeed, are not so dissimilar as appears. Wage-slavery and boredom seem to complete his outlook on the world. There are species which survive because of the feeling of disgust inspired by them: one is reluctant to set the heel firmly upon them, however thick may be one's boots. But when they are recognized as utterly noxious to humanity – the more so that they ape its form – then courage must be found, or, rather, nausea must be swallowed. May God send us a Saint George!

IV

It is notorious that all genius is accompanied by vice. Almost always this takes the form of sexual extravagance. It is to be observed that deficiency, as in the cases of Carlyle and Ruskin, is to be reckoned as extravagance. At least the word abnormalcy will fit all cases. Farther, we see that in a very large number of great men there has also been indulgence in drink or drugs. There are whole periods when practically every great man has been thus marked, and these periods are those during which the heroic spirit has died out of their nation, and the burgeois is apparently triumphant.

In this case the cause is evidently the horror of life induced in the artist by the contemplation of his surroundings. He must find another world, no matter at what cost.

Consider the end of the eighteenth century. In France the men of genius are made, so to speak, possible, by the Revolution. In England, under Castlereagh, we find Blake lost to humanity in mysticism, Shelley and Byron exiles, Coleridge taking refuge in opium, Keats sinking under the weight of circumstance, Wordsworth forced to sell his soul, while the enemy, in the persons of Southey and Moore, triumphantly holds sway.

The poetically similar period in France is 1850 to 1870. Hugo is in exile, and all his brethren are given to absinthe or to hashish or to opium.

There is however another consideration more important. There are some men who possess the understanding of the City of God, and know not the keys; or, if they possess them, have not force to turn them in the wards. Such men often seek to win heaven by forged credentials. Just so a youth who desires love is too often deceived by simulacra, embraces Lydia thinking her to be Lalage.

But the greatest men of all suffer neither the limitations of the former class nor the illusions of the latter. Yet we find them equally given to what is apparently indulgence. Lombroso has foolishly sought to find the source of this in madness – as if insanity could scale the peaks of Progress while Reason recoiled from the bergschrund. The explanation is far otherwise. Imagine to yourself the mental state of him who inherits or attains the full consciousness of the artist, that is to say, the divine consciousness.

He finds himself unutterably lonely, and he must steel himself to endure it. All his peers are dead long since! Even if he find an equal upon earth, there can scarcely be companionship, hardly more than the far courtesy of king to king.

There are no twin souls in genius.

Good – he can reconcile himself to the scorn of the world. But yet he feels with anguish his duty towards it. It is therefore essential to him to be human.

Now the divine consciousness is not full flowered in youth. The newness of the objective world preoccupies the soul for many years. It is only as each illusion vanishes before the magic of the master that he gains more and more the power to dwell in the world of Reality. And with this comes the terrible temptation – the desire to enter and enjoy rather than remain among men and suffer their illusions. Yet, since the sole purpose of the incarnation of such a Master was to help humanity, they must make the supreme renunciation. It is the problem of the dreadful bridge of Islam, Al Sirak – the razor-edge will cut the unwary foot, yet it must be trodden firmly, or the traveler will fall to the abyss. I dare not sit in the Old Absinthe House forever, wrapped in the ineffable delight of the Beatific Vision. I must write this essay, that men may thereby come at last to understand true things. But the operation of the creative godhead is not enough. Art is itself too near the reality which must be renounced for a season.

Therefore his work is also part of his temptation; the genius feels himself slipping constantly heavenward. The gravitation of eternity draws him. He is like a ship torn by the tempest from the harbor where the master must needs take on new passengers to the Happy Isles. So he must throw out anchors and the only holding is the mire! Thus in order to maintain the equilibrium of sanity, the artist is obliged to seek fellowship with the grossest of mankind.

Like Lord Dunsany or Augustus John, today, or like Teniers or old, he may love to sit in taverns where sailors frequent; or he may wander the country with Gypsies, or he may form liaisons with the vilest men and women. Edward Fitzgerald would see an illiterate fisherman and spend weeks in his company.

Verlaine made associates of Rimbaud and Bibi la Puree. Shakespeare consorted with the Earls of Pembroke and Southampton. Marlowe was actually killed during a brawl in a low tavern. And when we consider the sex-relation, it is hard to mention a genius who had a wife or mistress of even tolerable good character. If he had one, he would be sure to neglect her for a Vampire or a Shrew. A good woman is too near that heaven of Reality which he is sworn to renounce!

VI

Ah! the Green Goddess! What is the fascination that makes her so adorable and so terrible? Do you know that French sonnet 'La legende de l'absinthe?' He must have loved it well, that poet. Here are his witnesses.

> Apollon, qui pleurait le trepas d'Hyacinthe,
> Ne voulait pas ceder la victoire a la mort.
> Il fallait que son ame, adepte de l'essor,
> Trouvat pour la beaute une alchemie plus sainte.
> Donc de sa main celeste il epuise, il ereinte
> Les dons les plus subtils de la divine Flore.
> Leurs corps brises souspirent une exhalaison d'or
> Dont il nous recueillait la goutte de – l'Absinthe!
> Aux cavernes blotties, aux palis petillants,
> Par un, par deux, buvez ce breuvage d'aimant!
> Car c'est un sortilege, un propos de dictame,
> Ce vin d'opale pale avortit la misere,
> Ouvre de la beaute l'intime sanctuaire
> Ensorcelle mon coeur, extasie mort ame!

What is there in absinthe that makes it a separate cult? The effects of its abuse are totally distinct from those of other stimulants. Even in ruin and in degradation it remains a thing apart: its victims wear a ghastly aureole all their own, and in their peculiar hell yet gloat with a sinister perversion of pride that they are not as other men.

But we are not to reckon up the uses of a thing by contemplating the wreckage of its abuse. We do not curse the sea because of occasional disasters to our marines, or refuse axes to our woodsmen because we sympathize with Charles the First or Louis the Sixteenth. So therefore as special vices and dangers pertinent to absinthe, so also do graces and virtues that adorn no other liquor.

The word is from the Greek apsinthion. It means 'undrinkable' or, according to some authorities, 'undelightful.' In either case, strange paradox! No: for the wormwood draught itself were bitter beyond human endurance; it must be aromatized and mellowed with other herbs.

Chief among these is the gracious Melissa, of which the great Paracelsus thought so highly that he incorporated it as the preparation of his Ens Melissa Vitae, which he expected to be an elixir of life and a cure for all diseases, but which in his hands never came to perfection.

Then also there are added mint, anise, fennel and hyssop, all holy herbs familiar to all from the Treasury of Hebrew Scripture. And there is even the sacred marjoram which renders man both chaste and passionate; the tender green angelica stalks also infused in this most mystic of concoctions; for like the artemisia absinthium itself it is a plant of Diana, and gives the purity and lucidity, with a touch of the madness, of the Moon; and above all there is the Dittany of Crete of which the eastern Sages say that one flower hath more puissance in high magic than all the other gifts of all the gardens of the world.

It is as if the first diviner of absinthe had been indeed a magician intent upon a combination of sacred drugs which should cleanse, fortify and perfume the human soul.

And it is no doubt that in the due employment of this liquor such effects are easy to obtain. A single glass seems to render the breathing freer, the spirit lighter, the heart more ardent, soul and mind alike more capable of executing the great task of doing that particular work in the world which the Father may have sent them to perform. Food itself loses its gross qualities in the presence of absinthe and becomes even as manna, operating the sacrament of nutrition without bodily disturbance.

Let then the pilgrim enter reverently the shrine, and drink his absinthe as a stirrup-cup; for in the right conception of this life as an ordeal of chivalry lies the foundation of every perfection of philosophy. 'Whatsoever ye do, whether ye eat or drink, do all to the glory of God!' applies with singular force to the absintheur. So may he come victorious from the battle of life to be received with tender kisses by some green-robed archangel, and crowned with mystic vervain in the Emerald Gateway of the Golden City of God.

Extract from *Oscar Wilde,*
His Life and Confessions (1916)

FRANK HARRIS

A short yet wonderful recollection of the 'Beardsley years' of the mid-1890s
– featuring orchids, Baudelaire, Beardsley, Wilde and, of course, absinthe.

Aubrey Beardsley's genius had taken London by storm. At seventeen or eighteen this auburn-haired, blue-eyed, fragile looking youth had reached maturity with his astounding talent, a talent which would have given him position and wealth in any other country. In perfection of line his drawings were superior to anything we possess. But the curious thing about the boy was that he expressed the passions of pride and lust and cruelty more intensely even than Rops, more spontaneously than anyone who ever held pencil. Beardsley's precocity was simply marvelous. He seemed to have an intuitive understanding not only of his own art but of every art and craft, and it was some time before one realized that he attained this miraculous virtuosity by an absolute disdain for every other form of human endeavor. He knew nothing of the great general or millionaire or man of science, and he cared as little for them as for fishermen or bus-drivers. The current of his talent ran narrow between stone banks, so to speak; it was the bold assertion of it that interested Oscar.

One phase of Beardsley's extraordinary development may be recorded here. When I first met him his letters, and even his talk sometimes, were curiously youthful and immature, lacking altogether the personal note of his drawings. As soon as this was noticed he took the bull by the horns and pretended that his style in writing was out of date; he wished us to believe that he hesitated to shock us with his 'archaic sympathies.' Of course we laughed and challenged him to reveal himself. Shortly afterwards I got an article from him written with curious felicity of phrase, in modish polite eighteenth-century English. He had reached personal expression in a new medium in a month or so, and apparently without effort. It was Beardsley's writing that first won Oscar to recognition of his talent, and for a while he seemed vaguely interested in what he called his 'orchid-like personality.'

They were both at lunch one day when Oscar declared that he could drink nothing but absinthe when Beardsley was present.

'Absinthe,' he said, 'is to all other drinks what Aubrey's drawings are to other pictures; it stands alone; it is like nothing else; it shimmers like southern twilight in opalescent colouring; it has about it the seduction of strange sins. It is stronger than any other spirit and brings out the subconscious self in man. It is just like your drawings, Aubrey; it gets on one's nerves and is cruel.

'Baudelaire called his poems *Fleurs du Mal*, I shall call your drawings *Fleurs du Péché* – flowers of sin.

'When I have before me one of your drawings I want to drink absinthe, which changes color like jade in sunlight and makes the senses thrall, and then I can live myself back in imperial Rome, in the Rome of the later Caesars.'

'Dedicatory Sonnet' (1885)

JOHN BARLAS

A whirlpool of hallucinatory visions from John Barlas.

This Haschish dream, this cup-rose heavy-leaning
   With opiums weight, this drunkenness of soul,
   Bizarre, grotesque, satiric, with strange scroll
Of flaunting fancy's wildest foliage screening
No plashy depths of philosophic meaning,
   Scoffing, believing, laughing at life's dole,
   From heart that bleeds the while to death's dear goal,
   Take, friend – my own, from no man's field a gleaning.

For I have made myself a clean new mould
   To pour my fancies in, of mad burlesque,
   Yet full of death withal as charnel air.
I first of men have carved in fancy's gold
   So queer a pagod freaked in fancy's gold,
   Though treading Wagner's ground twixt Goethe
   and Baudelaire.

'Nerves' (1895)

ARTHUR SYMONS

'Sensitivity', 'nerves' and 'hysteria' were terms popularised in nineteenth-century medical literature, as doctors groped towards the recognition of mental health problems (and sought to maintain their power over the female population). Besides women, poets, artists and effeminate men were seen as especially at-risk for these peculiar symptoms, with decadence a most terrible catalyst. Arthur Symons succumbed to his own 'nerves' in 1908 when he suffered a mental breakdown from which he never recovered.

The modern malady of love is nerves.
Love, once a simple madness, now observes
The stages of his passionate disease,
And is twice sorrowful because he sees,
Inch by inch entering, the fatal knife.
O health of simple minds, give me your life,
And let me, for one midnight, cease to hear
The clock for ever ticking in my ear,
The clock that tells the minutes in my brain.
It is not love, nor love's despair, this pain
That shoots a witless, keener pang across
The simple agony of love and loss.
Nerves, nerves! O folly of a child who dreams
Of heaven, and, waking in the darkness, screams.

Extract from *The Race Of Orven* (1895)

M. P. SHIEL

Shiel's Prince Zaleski stories are a truly bizarre marriage of decadence and crime fiction. Zaleski retires from the world to his crumbling manor in order to smoke hashish and contemplate his objets d'art. *Occasionally he is roused from his ennui long enough to help solve a murder, which he accomplishes through drug-fuelled meditation rather than do something as tiresome as leave the house to investigate.*

Never without grief and pain could I remember the fate of Prince Zaleski – victim of a too importunate, too unfortunate Love, which the fulgor of the throne itself could not abash; exile perforce from his native land, and voluntary exile from the rest of men! Having renounced the world, over which, lurid and inscrutable as a falling star, he had passed, the world quickly ceased to wonder at him; and even I, to whom, more than to another, the workings of that just and passionate mind had been revealed, half forgot him in the rush of things.

But during the time that what was called the 'Pharanx labyrinth' was exercising many of the heaviest brains in the land, my thought turned repeatedly to him; and even when the affair had passed from the general attention, a bright day in Spring, combined perhaps with a latent mistrust of the *dénoûment* of that dark plot, drew me to his place of hermitage.

I reached the gloomy abode of my friend as the sun set. It was a vast palace of the older world standing lonely in the midst of woodland, and approached by a sombre avenue of poplars and cypresses, through which the sunlight hardly pierced. Up this I passed, and seeking out the deserted stables (which I found all too dilapidated to afford shelter) finally put up my *calèche* in the ruined sacristy of an old Dominican chapel, and turned my mare loose to browse for the night on a paddock behind the domain.

As I pushed back the open front door and entered the mansion, I could not but wonder at the saturnine fancy that had led this wayward man to select a brooding-place so desolate for the passage of his days. I regarded it as a vast tomb of Mausolus in which lay deep sepulchred how much genius, culture, brilliancy, power! The hall was constructed in the manner of a Roman *atrium*, and from the oblong pool of turgid water in the centre a troop of fat and otiose rats fled weakly squealing at my approach. I mounted by broken marble steps to the corridors running round the open space, and thence pursued my way through a mazeland of apartments – suite upon suite – along many a length of passage, up and down many stairs. Dust-clouds rose from the uncarpeted floors and choked me; incontinent Echo coughed answering *ricochets* to my footsteps in the gathering darkness, and added emphasis to the funereal gloom of the dwelling. Nowhere was there a vestige of furniture – nowhere a trace of human life.

After a long interval I came, in a remote tower of the building and near its utmost summit, to a richly-carpeted passage, from the ceiling of which three mosaic lamps shed dim violet, scarlet and pale-rose lights around. At the end I perceived two figures standing as if in silent guard on each side of a door tapestried with the python's skin. One was a post-replica in Parian marble of the nude Aphrodite of Cnidus; in the other I recognised the gigantic form of the negro Ham, the prince's only attendant, whose fierce, and glistening, and ebon visage broadened into a grin of intelligence as I came nearer. Nodding to him, I pushed without ceremony into Zaleski's apartment.

The room was not a large one, but lofty. Even in the semi-darkness of the very faint greenish lustre radiated from an open censerlike *lampas* of fretted gold in the centre of the domed encausted roof, a certain incongruity of barbaric gorgeousness in the furnishing filled me with amazement. The air was heavy with the scented odour of this light, and the fumes of the narcotic *cannabis sativa* – the base of the *bhang* of the Mohammedans – in which I knew it to be the habit of my friend to assuage himself. The hangings were of wine-coloured velvet, heavy, gold-fringed and embroidered at Nurshedabad. All the world knew Prince Zaleski to be a consummate *cognoscente* – a profound amateur – as well as a savant and a thinker; but I was, nevertheless, astounded at the mere multitudinousness of the curios he had contrived to crowd into the space around him. Side by side rested a palaeolithic implement, a Chinese 'wise man,' a Gnostic gem, an amphora of Graeco-Etruscan work. The general effect was a *bizarrerie* of half-weird sheen and gloom. Flemish sepulchral brasses companied strangely with runic tablets, miniature paintings, a winged bull, Tamil scriptures on lacquered leaves of the talipot, mediaeval reliquaries richly gemmed, Brahmin gods. One whole side of the room was occupied by an organ whose thunder in that circumscribed place must have set all these relics of dead epochs clashing and jingling in fantastic dances. As I entered, the vaporous atmosphere was palpitating to the low, liquid tinkling of an invisible musical box. The prince reclined on a couch from which a draping of cloth-of-silver rolled torrent over the floor. Beside him, stretched in its open sarcophagus which rested on three brazen trestles, lay the mummy of an ancient Memphian, from the upper part of which the brown cerements had rotted or been rent, leaving the hideousness of the naked, grinning countenance exposed to view.

Discarding his gemmed chibouque and an old vellum reprint of Anacreon, Zaleski rose hastily and greeted me with warmth, muttering at the same time some commonplace about his 'pleasure' and the 'unexpectedness' of my visit. He then gave orders to Ham to prepare me a bed in one of the adjoining chambers. We passed the greater part of the night in a delightful stream of that somnolent and half-mystic talk which Prince Zaleski alone could initiate and sustain, during which he repeatedly pressed on me a concoction of Indian hemp resembling *hashish*, prepared by his own hands, and quite innocuous. It was after a simple breakfast the next morning that I entered on the subject which was partly the occasion of my visit. He lay back on his couch, volumed in a Turkish *beneesh*, and listened to me, a little wearily perhaps at first, with woven fingers, and the pale inverted eyes of old anchorites and astrologers, the moony greenish light falling on his always wan features.

'Non sum qualis eram bonae sub regno Cynarae' (1894)

ERNEST DOWSON

Last night, ah, yesternight, betwixt her lips and mine
There fell thy shadow, Cynara! thy breath was shed
Upon my soul between the kisses and the wine;
And I was desolate and sick of an old passion,
Yea, I was desolate and bowed my head:
I have been faithful to thee, Cynara! in my fashion.

All night upon mine heart I felt her warm heart beat,
Night-long within mine arms in love and sleep she lay;
Surely the kisses of her bought red mouth were sweet;
But I was desolate and sick of an old passion,
When I awoke and found the dawn was grey:
I have been faithful to thee, Cynara! in my fashion.

I have forgot much, Cynara! gone with the wind,
Flung roses, roses riotously with the throng,
Dancing, to put thy pale, lost lilies out of mind,
But I was desolate and sick of an old passion,
Yea, all the time, because the dance was long:
I have been faithful to thee, Cynara! in my fashion.

I cried for madder music and for stronger wine,
But when the feast is finished and the lamps expire,
Then falls thy shadow, Cynara! the night is thine;
And I am desolate and sick of an old passion,
Yea, hungry for the lips of my desire:
I have been faithful to thee, Cynara! in my fashion.

'To One in Bedlam' (1892)

ERNEST DOWSON

Decadence was explicitly considered a form of mental disease by Nordau and the popular press, but its adherents often flirted quite openly with madness, interested in the intoxication and inspiration that altered states could offer. It is often considered naive to romanticise the connection between genius and insanity, but Dowson seems painfully intent on doing just that in this short poem.

(*For Henry Davray*)
With delicate, mad hands, behind his sordid bars,
Surely he hath his posies, which they tear and twine;
Those scentless wisps of straw, that miserably line
His strait, caged universe, whereat the dull world stares,

Pedant and pityful. O, how his rapt gaze wars
With their stupidity! Know they what dreams divine
Lift his long, laughing reveries like enchanted wine,
And make his melancholy germane to the stars?

O lamentable brother! if those pity thee,
Am I not fain of all thy lone eyes promise me;
Half a fool's kingdom, far from men who sow and reap,
All their days, vanity? Better than mortal flowers,
Thy moon-kissed roses seem: better than love or sleep,
The star-crowned solitude of thine oblivious hours!

Extract from *Letters to the Sphinx from Oscar Wilde* (1930)

ADA LEVERSON

Ada Leverson was a great friend of Oscar Wilde and a renowned wit herself, although her popularity has waned over the years. Her Letters to the Sphinx from Oscar Wilde *is full of funny and intriguing recollections.*

One day he was talking of the effect of absinthe. 'After the first glass, you see things as you wish they were. After the second, you see them as they are not. Finally you see things as they really are, and that is the most horrible thing in the world.'

'How do you mean?'

'I mean disassociated. Take a top-hat! You think you see it as it really is. But you don't, because you associate it with other things and ideas. If you had never heard of one before, suddenly saw it alone, you'd be frightened, or laugh. That is the effect absinthe has, and that is why it drives men mad.

'Three nights I sat up all night drinking absinthe, and thinking that I was singularly clear-headed and sane. The waiter came in and began watering the sawdust. The most wonderful flowers, tulips, lilies and roses sprang up and made a garden of the cafe. "Don't you see them?" I said to him. "Mais non, Monsieur; il n'y a rien."

'In Bohemia' (1896)

ARTHUR SYMONS

The night is over, the morning dawns, and all seems but a dream. Every generation spends at least a little bit of time 'In Bohemia', but few describe it with as much pathos and poignancy as Symons does here.

Dawn blinds and flaring gas within,
    And wine, and women, and cigars;
Without, the city's heedless din;
    Above, the white unheeding stars.

And we, alike from each remote,
    The world that works, the heaven that waits,
Con our brief pleasures o'er by rote,
    The favourite pastime of the Fates.

We smoke, to fancy that we dream,
    And drink, a moment's joy to prove,
And fain would love, and only seem
    To love because we cannot love.

Draw back the blinds, put out the light:
    'Tis morning, let the daylight come.
God! how the women's checks are white,
    And how the sunlight strikes us dumb!

'The Opium-Smoker' (1892)

ARTHUR SYMONS

Like the drug itself, the poem seduces so gently that the reader is caught surprised by its deathly embrace.

I am engulfed, and drown deliciously.
Soft music like a perfume, and sweet light
Golden with audible odours exquisite,
Swathe me with cerements for eternity.
Time is no more. I pause and yet I flee.
A million ages wrap me round with night.
I drain a million ages of delight.
I hold the future in my memory.

Also I have this garret which I rent,
This bed of straw, and this that was a chair,
This worn-out body like a tattered tent,
This crust, of which the rats have eaten part,
This pipe of opium; rage, remorse, despair;
This soul at pawn and this delirious heart.

Extracts from 'The Effects of Absinthe' (1906)

EMMA E. WALKER, MD

By the fin *of the* fin de siècle, *absinthe had inspired such moral panic that it was banned in America, France and most of Europe. It was claimed to cause all manner of ills, but whether the threat posed by absinthe was any worse than alcohol in general is debatable. Supposedly the wormwood is highly toxic, but subsequent pharmacological tests have proved that while large doses of wormwood oil can cause convulsions, the amount used in absinthe is incredibly safe. The only thing in absinthe that is definitely dangerous is, rather boringly, the alcohol. Furthermore, the psychoactive effects of wormwood seem to have been grossly exaggerated. Still, for a flavour of the hysteria, enjoy the following excerpts from a 1906 medical journal, which attempts restraint but occasionally indulges in salacious commentary.*

Medical Record, Volume 70, 13 October 1906

France as a nation has become so roused to the danger of alcohol and the essences, especially absinthe, which are in such common use in that country, that on December 29, 1900, the French government requested the Academy of Medicine to determine the comparative toxicity of the various alcoholic beverages in use with a view to proscribing the ones most dangerous to health. After an investigation it was suggested by one of the committee that absinthe alone be put into the forbidden list.

In France absinthe is known as the 'scourge,' the 'plague,' the 'enemy,' and the 'queen of poisons.' Absinthe is a liquor of an emerald green color, consisting of from 47 to 80 per cent, of alcohol, highly flavored with the aromatics, wormwood, anise, fennel, coriander, calamus aromaticus, hyssop, and marjoram. The special variety of this drink depends upon the proportions and kinds of these flavors composing it. Its quality will also depend upon the quality of its constituents. Since any unpleasant taste may be easily concealed by the strong aromatic used, the alcohol employed in this liquor is frequently very impure.

Absinthe heads the list of toxic essences. The ordinary absinthe contains a far larger percentage of alcohol than does whiskey. Consequently its toxic effects are far greater than are those of whiskey, for to the increased amount of alcohol there is added the deadly wormwood.

In France, according to the law of March 26, 1872, it was declared that the commerce and sale of the essence of absinthe ought to be carried on by the pharmacists according to the law on the sale of poisons.

Absinthe, *Artemisia absinthium,* is the common wormwood, the bitterness of which has passed into a proverb. Absinthe is quoted to contain only one third of 1 per cent, of the oil of wormwood, to which are due the characteristic effects of the beverage. The bitter principle of absinthium, *absinthin,* is a narcotic poison. The coloring matters used in absinthe are often very deleterious; in fact not infrequently copper salts have been used in order to produce the green color.

Absinthe is chiefly used in France, and especially in Paris. It was introduced there after the Algerian war of 1844–7 by the soldiers, who, on their campaign, had been advised to mix absinthe with their wine as a febrifuge. The use of absinthe rapidly increased in France with such disastrous results that it has been described by French physicians as constituting a graver danger to the public than alcohol itself.

The habit of absinthe drinking is a most insidious one, and when it is once indulged it seems almost impossible to break. Thirst is more exacting than hunger. It is often a purely imaginary sensation. 'Arrived at a morbid degree, the passion for drink is not only a vice which blights equally the reason, morality and- justice, but is a veritable mental malady' (Paul Jolly). 'The poisonous and inebriating effects produced in those who drink the liqueur of absinthe or cream of absinthe is undoubtedly due more to the wormwood than to the alcohol' (Trousseau and Pideaux).

From the point of view of absinthe epilepsy, it is known that in many epileptics the sexual instinct is most intense. It may be that the cerebral changes incident to the epileptic outbreak cause an abnormal stimulation of the sexual instinct. In many cases this excitement is not active during

intervals, but is shown only in connection with the epileptic attack or in the post-epileptic period. 'Nobody questions the harm wrought by wormwood in its role of servant to human debauchery.' Through the entire career of chronic alcoholism 'runs the thread of mental degradation involving moral obliquity.' The poison produces a physical degradation, which is followed by mental and moral palsy. Lying becomes second nature; conscience is deadened. Kerr says that 'the sexual function is responsible for much periodical excitation of inebriety.'

The delirious attacks of absinthe develop suddenly, just as 'after the administration of certain poisons, of hyoscyamus, belladonna, or stramonium, and this rapidity in the development of the intellectual disturbances is one of the distinctive characteristics distinguishing the action of absinthe and that of alcohol.'

Robinovitch says that in the case of the absintheur 'the whole clinical tableau of alcoholic poisoning seems to be condensed, so to speak, within the shortest possible space of time. The excitation of the senses, the delirium, the muscular cramps, the dizziness, vertigo, and finally the true epileptic convulsions set in, and follow one another in rapid succession.

Where years are necessary for alcoholic morbid changes to be expressed clinically by epileptiform attacks, one year or even less, suffices to bring about true epileptic attacks by the abuse of absinthe.'

Absinthism differs in various ways from alcoholism. In the former are manifested hallucinations and terrible dreams, enfeeblement of the intellect, and stupor, all of which may develop rapidly without any muscular tremor. If this tremor does exist, it is usually confined to the upper extremities. Absintheurs are restless at night. They suffer from nightmare, nausea, lack of appetite, vomiting, mental dullness, and sometimes delirium or mania. Mental deterioration progresses. The power of concentration of memory is impaired, and the patient loses his will power. He becomes indifferent to the welfare of both himself and his family and friends. Instead of the simple muscular tremor of delirium tremens, as is seen in the alcoholic, the epileptic fit is seen in the absinthe drinker. The fit recurs from time to time. If the habit is overcome during the early stages the fits cease. But if the indulgence is continued the intellect is permanently deranged and paralysis and death result. The morbid changes which develop vary according to the individual predisposition. Sometimes the fits are more like an attack of hysteria. Absintheurs have hallucinations of sight and hearing which do not represent a condition like delirium tremens. The victims of this habit become absolute physical and moral wrecks.

'Absinthia Taetra' (1899)

ERNEST DOWSON

Reflections of a devoted absintheur.

Green changed to white, emerald to an opal: nothing was changed.

The man let the water trickle gently into his glass, and as the green clouded, a mist fell from his mind.

Then he drank opaline.

Memories and terrors beset him. The past tore after him like a panther and through the blackness of the present he saw the luminous tiger eyes of the things to be.

But he drank opaline.

And that obscure night of the soul, and the valley of humiliation, through which he stumbled were forgotten. He saw blue vistas of undiscovered countries, high prospects and a quiet, caressing sea. The past shed its perfume over him, to-day held his hand as it were a little child, and to-morrow shone like a white star: nothing was changed.

He drank opaline.

The man had known the obscure night of the soul, and lay even now in the valley of humiliation; and the tiger menace of the things to be was red in the skies. But for a little while he had forgotten.

Green changed to white, emerald to an opal: nothing was changed.

"Giving heed to seducing spirits."—I TIMOTHY, iv. I.

4

Giving Heed to Seducing Spirits
—SPIRITUALITY

'Science is all very well in its way,' said I; 'and of course it's an inestimable
advantage to inhabit this so-called nineteenth century;
but the mediaeval want of science was far more picturesque.
The once universal belief in charms and portents, in wandering saints,
and fighting fairies, must have lent an interest to life which
these prosaic days sadly lack.'
Ella D'Arcy, *White Magic*

Extract from 'The White People' (1899)

ARTHUR MACHEN

In 1890s Britain, intense spirituality usually manifested itself as a particularly aesthetic form of Catholicism, but several decadent writers would flirt more openly with paganism and the occult. Machen's The Great God Pan *is a prime example, but the prologue to his* The White People *is an enjoyable and illuminating discussion of Sin (a key concern of the decadent), with a healthy dose of bibliophilia.*

Prologue

'Sorcery and sanctity,' said Ambrose, 'these are the only realities. Each is an ecstasy, a withdrawal from the common life.'

Cotgrave listened, interested. He had been brought by a friend to this mouldering house in a northern suburb, through an old garden to the room where Ambrose the recluse dozed and dreamed over his books.

'Yes,' he went on, 'magic is justified of her children. There are many, I think, who eat dry crusts and drink water, with a joy infinitely sharper than anything within the experience of the "practical" epicure.'

'You are speaking of the saints?'

'Yes, and of the sinners, too. I think you are falling into the very general error of confining the spiritual world to the supremely good; but the supremely wicked, necessarily, have their portion in it. The merely carnal, sensual man can no more be a great sinner than he can be a great saint. Most of us are just indifferent, mixed-up creatures; we muddle through the world without realizing the meaning and the inner sense of things, and, consequently, our wickedness and our goodness are alike second-rate, unimportant.'

'And you think the great sinner, then, will be an ascetic, as well as the great saint?'

'Great people of all kinds forsake the imperfect copies and go to the perfect originals. I have no doubt but that many of the very highest among the saints have never done a "good action" (using the words in their ordinary sense). And, on the other hand, there have been those who have sounded the very depths of sin, who all their lives have never done an "ill deed."'

He went out of the room for a moment, and Cotgrave, in high delight, turned to his friend and thanked him for the introduction.

'He's grand,' he said. 'I never saw that kind of lunatic before.'

Ambrose returned with more whisky and helped the two men in a liberal manner. He abused the teetotal sect with ferocity, as he handed the seltzer, and pouring out a glass of water for himself, was about to resume his monologue, when Cotgrave broke in—

'I can't stand it, you know,' he said, 'your paradoxes are too monstrous. A man may be a great sinner and yet never do anything sinful! Come!'

'You're quite wrong,' said Ambrose. 'I never make paradoxes; I wish I could. I merely said that a man may have an exquisite taste in Romanée Conti, and yet never have even smelt four ale. That's all, and it's more like a truism than a paradox, isn't it? Your surprise at my remark is due to the fact that you haven't realized what sin is. Oh, yes, there is a sort of connexion between Sin with the capital letter, and actions which are commonly called sinful: with murder, theft, adultery, and so forth. Much the same connexion that there is between the A, B, C and fine literature. But I believe that the misconception – it is all but universal – arises in great measure from our looking at the matter through social spectacles. We think that a man who does evil to *us* and to his neighbours must be very evil. So he is, from a social standpoint; but can't you realize that Evil in its essence is a lonely thing, a passion of the solitary, individual soul? Really, the average murderer, *quâ* murderer, is not by any means a sinner in the true sense of the word. He is simply a wild beast that we have to get rid of to save our own necks from his knife. I should class him rather with tigers than with sinners.'

'It seems a little strange.'

'I think not. The murderer murders not from positive qualities, but

from negative ones; he lacks something which non-murderers possess. Evil, of course, is wholly positive – only it is on the wrong side. You may believe me that sin in its proper sense is very rare; it is probable that there have been far fewer sinners than saints. Yes, your standpoint is all very well for practical, social purposes; we are naturally inclined to think that a person who is very disagreeable to us must be a very great sinner! It is very disagreeable to have one's pocket picked, and we pronounce the thief to be a very great sinner. In truth, he is merely an undeveloped man. He cannot be a saint, of course; but he may be, and often is, an infinitely better creature than thousands who have never broken a single commandment. He is a great nuisance to *us*, I admit, and we very properly lock him up if we catch him; but between his troublesome and unsocial action and evil – Oh, the connexion is of the weakest.'

It was getting very late. The man who had brought Cotgrave had probably heard all this before, since he assisted with a bland and judicious smile, but Cotgrave began to think that his 'lunatic' was turning into a sage.

'Do you know,' he said, 'you interest me immensely? You think, then, that we do not understand the real nature of evil?'

'No, I don't think we do. We over-estimate it and we under-estimate it. We take the very numerous infractions of our social "bye-laws" – the very necessary and very proper regulations which keep the human company together – and we get frightened at the prevalence of "sin" and "evil." But this is really nonsense. Take theft, for example. Have you any *horror* at the thought of Robin Hood, of the Highland caterans of the seventeenth century, of the moss-troopers, of the company promoters of our day?

'Then, on the other hand, we underrate evil. We attach such an enormous importance to the "sin" of meddling with our pockets (and our wives) that we have quite forgotten the awfulness of real sin.'

'And what is sin?' said Cotgrave.

'I think I must reply to your question by another. What would your

feelings be, seriously, if your cat or your dog began to talk to you, and to dispute with you in human accents? You would be overwhelmed with horror. I am sure of it. And if the roses in your garden sang a weird song, you would go mad. And suppose the stones in the road began to swell and grow before your eyes, and if the pebble that you noticed at night had shot out stony blossoms in the morning?

'Well, these examples may give you some notion of what sin really is.'

'Look here,' said the third man, hitherto placid, 'you two seem pretty well wound up. But I'm going home. I've missed my tram, and I shall have to walk.'

Ambrose and Cotgrave seemed to settle down more profoundly when the other had gone out into the early misty morning and the pale light of the lamps.

'You astonish me,' said Cotgrave. 'I had never thought of that. If that is really so, one must turn everything upside down. Then the essence of sin really is—'

'In the taking of heaven by storm, it seems to me,' said Ambrose. 'It appears to me that it is simply an attempt to penetrate into another and higher sphere in a forbidden manner. You can understand why it is so rare. There are few, indeed, who wish to penetrate into other spheres, higher or lower, in ways allowed or forbidden. Men, in the mass, are amply content with life as they find it. Therefore there are few saints, and sinners (in the proper sense) are fewer still, and men of genius, who partake sometimes of each character, are rare also. Yes; on the whole, it is, perhaps, harder to be a great sinner than a great saint.'

'There is something profoundly unnatural about sin? Is that what you mean?'

'Exactly. Holiness requires as great, or almost as great, an effort; but holiness works on lines that were natural once; it is an effort to recover the ecstasy that was before the Fall. But sin is an effort to gain the ecstasy and the knowledge that pertain alone to angels and in making this effort man becomes a demon. I told you that the mere murderer is not *therefore* a sinner; that is true, but the sinner is sometimes a murderer. Gilles de Raiz is an instance. So you see that while the good and the evil are unnatural to man as he now is – to man the social, civilized being – evil is unnatural in a much deeper sense than good. The saint endeavours to recover a gift which he has lost; the sinner tries to obtain something which was never his. In brief, he repeats the Fall.'

'But are you a Catholic?' said Cotgrave.

'Yes; I am a member of the persecuted Anglican Church.'

'Then, how about those texts which seem to reckon as sin that which you would set down as a mere trivial dereliction?'

'Yes; but in one place the word "sorcerers" comes in the same sentence, doesn't it? That seems to me to give the key-note. Consider: can you imagine for a moment that a false statement which saves an innocent man's life is a sin? No; very good, then, it is not the mere liar who is excluded by those words; it is, above all, the "sorcerers" who use the material life, who use the failings incidental to material life as instruments to obtain their infinitely wicked ends. And let me tell you this: our higher senses are so blunted, we are so drenched with materialism, that we should probably fail to recognize real wickedness if we encountered it.'

'But shouldn't we experience a certain horror – a terror such as you hinted we would experience if a rose tree sang – in the mere presence of an evil man?'

'We should if we were natural: children and women feel this horror you speak of, even animals experience it. But with most of us convention and civilization and education have blinded and deafened and obscured the natural reason. No, sometimes we may recognize evil by its hatred of the good – one doesn't need much penetration to guess at the influence which dictated, quite unconsciously, the "Blackwood" review of Keats – but this is purely incidental; and, as a rule, I suspect that the Hierarchs of Tophet pass quite unnoticed, or, perhaps, in certain cases, as good but mistaken men.'

'But you used the word "unconscious" just now, of Keats' reviewers. Is wickedness ever unconscious?'

'Always. It must be so. It is like holiness and genius in this as in other points; it is a certain rapture or ecstasy of the soul; a transcendent effort to surpass the ordinary bounds. So, surpassing these, it surpasses also the

understanding, the faculty that takes note of that which comes before it. No, a man may be infinitely and horribly wicked and never suspect it But I tell you, evil in this, its certain and true sense, is rare, and I think it is growing rarer.'

'I am trying to get hold of it all,' said Cotgrave. 'From what you say, I gather that the true evil differs generically from that which we call evil?'

'Quite so. There is, no doubt, an analogy between the two; a resemblance such as enables us to use, quite legitimately, such terms as the "foot of the mountain" and the "leg of the table." And, sometimes, of course, the two speak, as it were, in the same language. The rough miner, or "puddler," the untrained, undeveloped "tiger-man," heated by a quart or two above his usual measure, comes home and kicks his irritating and injudicious wife to death. He is a murderer. And Gilles de Raiz was a murderer. But you see the gulf that separates the two? The "word," if I may so speak, is accidentally the same in each case, but the "meaning" is utterly different. It is flagrant "Hobson Jobson" to confuse the two, or rather, it is as if one supposed that Juggernaut and the Argonauts had something to do etymologically with one another. And no doubt the same weak likeness, or analogy, runs between all the "social" sins and the real spiritual sins, and in some cases, perhaps, the lesser may be "schoolmasters" to lead one on to the greater – from the shadow to the reality. If you are anything of a Theologian, you will see the importance of all this.'

'I am sorry to say,' remarked Cotgrave, 'that I have devoted very little of my time to theology. Indeed, I have often wondered on what grounds theologians have claimed the title of Science of Sciences for their favourite study; since the "theological" books I have looked into have always seemed to me to be concerned with feeble and obvious pieties, or with the kings of Israel and Judah. I do not care to hear about those kings.'

Ambrose grinned.

'We must try to avoid theological discussion,' he said. 'I perceive that you would be a bitter disputant. But perhaps the "dates of the kings" have as much to do with theology as the hobnails of the murderous puddler with evil.'

'Then, to return to our main subject, you think that sin is an esoteric, occult thing?'

'Yes. It is the infernal miracle as holiness is the supernal. Now and then it is raised to such a pitch that we entirely fail to suspect its existence; it is like the note of the great pedal pipes of the organ, which is so deep that we cannot hear it. In other cases it may lead to the lunatic asylum, or to still stranger issues. But you must never confuse it with mere social misdoing. Remember how the Apostle, speaking of the "other side," distinguishes between "charitable" actions and charity. And as one may give all one's goods to the poor, and yet lack charity; so, remember, one may avoid every crime and yet be a sinner.'

'Your psychology is very strange to me,' said Cotgrave, 'but I confess I like it, and I suppose that one might fairly deduce from your premisses the conclusion that the real sinner might very possibly strike the observer as a harmless personage enough?'

'Certainly, because the true evil has nothing to do with social life or social laws, or if it has, only incidentally and accidentally. It is a lonely passion of the soul – or a passion of the lonely soul – whichever you like. If, by chance, we understand it, and grasp its full significance, then, indeed, it will fill us with horror and with awe. But this emotion is widely distinguished from the fear and the disgust with which we regard the ordinary criminal, since this latter is largely or entirely founded on the regard which we have for our own skins or purses. We hate a murder, because we know that we should hate to be murdered, or to have any one that we like murdered. So, on the "other side," we venerate the saints, but we don't "like" them as well as our friends. Can you persuade yourself that you would have "enjoyed" St. Paul's company? Do you think that you and I would have "got on" with Sir Galahad?

'So with the sinners, as with the saints. If you met a very evil man, and recognized his evil; he would, no doubt, fill you with horror and awe; but there is no reason why you should "dislike" him. On the contrary, it is quite possible that if you could succeed in putting the sin out of your mind you might find the sinner capital company, and in a little while you might have to reason yourself back into horror. Still, how awful it is. If the roses and the lilies suddenly sang on this coming morning; if the furniture began to move in procession, as in De Maupassant's tale!'

'I am glad you have come back to that comparison,' said Cotgrave, 'because I wanted to ask you what it is that corresponds in humanity to these imaginary feats of inanimate things. In a word — what is sin? You have given me, I know, an abstract definition, but I should like a concrete example.'

'I told you it was very rare,' said Ambrose, who appeared willing to avoid the giving of a direct answer. 'The materialism of the age, which has done a good deal to suppress sanctity, has done perhaps more to suppress evil. We find the earth so very comfortable that we have no inclination either for ascents or descents. It would seem as if the scholar who decided to "specialize" in Tophet, would be reduced to purely antiquarian researches. No palæontologist could show you a *live* pterodactyl.'

'And yet you, I think, have "specialized," and I believe that your researches have descended to our modern times.'

'You are really interested, I see. Well, I confess, that I have dabbled a little, and if you like I can show you something that bears on the very curious subject we have been discussing.'

Ambrose took a candle and went away to a far, dim corner of the room. Cotgrave saw him open a venerable bureau that stood there, and from some secret recess he drew out a parcel, and came back to the window where they had been sitting.

Ambrose undid a wrapping of paper, and produced a green pocket-book.

'You will take care of it?' he said. 'Don't leave it lying about. It is one of the choicer pieces in my collection, and I should be very sorry if it were lost.'

He fondled the faded binding.

'I knew the girl who wrote this,' he said. 'When you read it, you will see how it illustrates the talk we have had to-night. There is a sequel, too, but I won't talk of that.

'There was an odd article in one of the reviews some months ago,' he began again, with the air of a man who changes the subject. 'It was written by a doctor – Dr. Coryn, I think, was the name. He says that a lady, watching her little girl playing at the drawing-room window, suddenly saw the heavy sash give way and fall on the child's fingers. The lady fainted, I think, but at any rate the doctor was summoned, and when he had dressed the child's wounded and maimed fingers he was summoned to the mother. She was groaning with pain, and it was found that three fingers of her hand, corresponding with those that had been injured on the child's hand, were swollen and inflamed, and later, in the doctor's language, purulent sloughing set in.'

Ambrose still handled delicately the green volume.

'Well, here it is,' he said at last, parting with difficulty, it seemed, from his treasure.

'You will bring it back as soon as you have read it,' he said, as they went out into the hall, into the old garden, faint with the odour of white lilies.

There was a broad red band in the east as Cotgrave turned to go, and from the high ground where he stood he saw that awful spectacle of London in a dream.

'Hymn to Lucifer' (*c.* 1900)

ALEISTER CROWLEY

Aleister Crowley's first collection of poetry was published in 1898
by Leonard Smithers, the 'publisher of the decadents', and he
forged links with several of Smithers's coterie. Much of the
supposedly satanic nature of decadence was a ruse adopted by
playful young writers, but Crowley took the joke far further than
anybody else...

Ware, nor of good nor ill, what aim hath act?
Without its climax, death, what savour hath
Life? an impeccable machine, exact
He paces an inane and pointless path
To glut brute appetites, his sole content
How tedious were he fit to comprehend
Himself! More, this our noble element
Of fire in nature, love in spirit, unkenned
Life hath no spring, no axle, and no end.

His body a bloody-ruby radiant
With noble passion, sun-souled Lucifer
Swept through the dawn colossal, swift aslant
On Eden's imbecile perimeter.
He blessed nonentity with every curse
And spiced with sorrow the dull soul of sense,
Breathed life into the sterile universe,
With Love and Knowledge drove out innocence
The Key of Joy is disobedience.

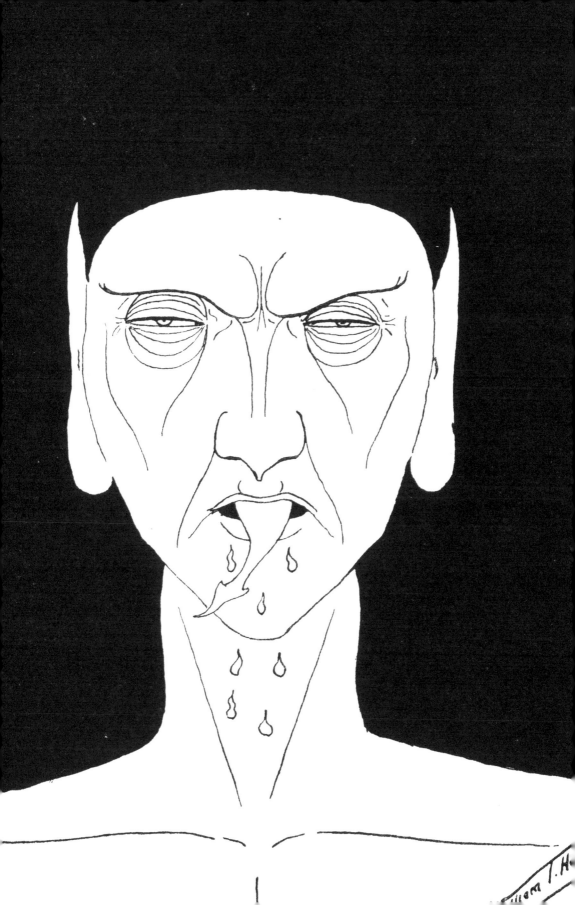

Extract from 'Enoch Soames' (1916)

MAX BEERBOHM

Enoch Soames is a complex parody of the 1890s literary world, in which Beerbohm recalls his experiences with the eponymous character, supposedly an overlooked poet. The short story features numerous real figures of the age and operates as a very funny send-up of their youthful pretentiousness. Absinthe, impenetrable poetry and some casual diabolism feature heavily.

In the summer term of '93 a bolt from the blue flashed down on Oxford. It drove deep; it hurtlingly embedded itself in the soil. Dons and undergraduates stood around, rather pale, discussing nothing but it. Whence came it, this meteorite? From Paris. Its name? Will Rothenstein. Its aim? To do a series of twenty-four portraits in lithograph. These were to be published from the Bodley Head, London. The matter was urgent. Already the warden of A, and the master of B, and the Regius Professor of C had meekly 'sat.' Dignified and doddering old men who had never consented to sit to any one could not withstand this dynamic little stranger. He did not sue; he invited: he did not invite; he commanded. He was twenty-one years old. He wore spectacles that flashed more than any other pair ever seen. He was a wit. He was brimful of ideas. He knew Whistler. He knew Daudet and the Goncourts. He knew every one in Paris. He knew them all by heart. He was Paris in Oxford. It was whispered that, so soon as he had polished off his selection of dons, he was going to include a few undergraduates. It was a proud day for me when I — I was included. I liked Rothenstein not less than I feared him; and there arose between us a friendship that has grown ever warmer, and been more and more valued by me, with every passing year.

At the end of term he settled in, or, rather, meteoritically into, London. It was to him I owed my first knowledge of that forever-enchanting little world-in-itself, Chelsea, and my first acquaintance with Walter Sickert and other August elders who dwelt there. It was Rothenstein that took me to see, in Cambridge Street, Pimlico, a young man whose drawings were already famous among the few – Aubrey Beardsley by name. With Rothenstein I paid my first visit to the Bodley Head. By him I was inducted into another haunt of intellect and daring, the domino-room of the Café Royal.

There, on that October evening – there, in that exuberant vista of gilding and crimson velvet set amidst all those opposing mirrors and upholding caryatids, with fumes of tobacco ever rising to the painted and pagan ceiling, and with the hum of presumably cynical conversation broken into so sharply now and again by the clatter of dominoes shuffled on marble tables, I drew a deep breath and, 'This indeed,' said I to myself, 'is life!' (Forgive me that theory. Remember the waging of even the South African War was not yet.)

It was the hour before dinner. We drank vermuth. Those who knew Rothenstein were pointing him out to those who knew him only by name. Men were constantly coming in through the swing-doors and wandering slowly up and down in search of vacant tables or of tables occupied by friends. One of these rovers interested me because I was sure he wanted to catch Rothenstein's eye. He had twice passed our table, with a hesitating look; but Rothenstein, in the thick of a disquisition on Puvis de Chavannes, had not seen him. He was a stooping, shambling person, rather tall, very pale, with longish and brownish hair. He had a thin, vague beard, or, rather, he had a chin on which a large number of hairs weakly curled and clustered to cover its retreat. He was an odd-looking person; but in the nineties odd apparitions were more frequent, I think, than they are now. The young writers of that era – and I was sure this man was a writer – strove earnestly to be distinct in aspect. This man had striven unsuccessfully. He wore a soft black hat of clerical kind, but of Bohemian intention, and a gray waterproof cape which, perhaps because it was waterproof, failed to be romantic. I decided that 'dim' was the mot juste for him. I had already essayed to write, and was immensely keen on the mot juste , that Holy Grail of the period.

The dim man was now again approaching our table, and this time he made up his mind to pause in front of it.

'You don't remember me,' he said in a toneless voice.

Rothenstein brightly focused him.

'Yes, I do,' he replied after a moment, with pride rather than effusion – pride in a retentive memory. 'Edwin Soames.'

'Enoch Soames,' said Enoch.

'Enoch Soames,' repeated Rothenstein in a tone implying that it was enough to have hit on the surname. 'We met in Paris a few times when you were living there. We met at the Café Groche.'

'And I came to your studio once.'

'Oh, yes; I was sorry I was out.'

'But you were in. You showed me some of your paintings, you know. I hear you're in Chelsea now.'

'Yes.'

I almost wondered that Mr. Soames did not, after this monosyllable, pass along. He stood patiently there, rather like a dumb animal, rather like a donkey looking over a gate. A sad figure, his. It occurred to me that 'hungry' was perhaps the mot juste for him; but – hungry for what? He looked as if he had little appetite for anything. I was sorry for him; and Rothenstein, though he had not invited him to Chelsea, did ask him to sit down and have something to drink.

Seated, he was more self-assertive. He flung back the wings of his cape with a gesture which, had not those wings been waterproof, might have seemed to hurl defiance at things in general. And he ordered an absinthe. 'Je me tiens toujours fidèle,' he told Rothenstein, 'à la sorcière glauque.'

'It is bad for you,' said Rothenstein, dryly.

'Nothing is bad for one,' answered Soames. 'Dans ce monde il n'y a ni bien ni mal.'

'Nothing good and nothing bad? How do you mean?'

'I explained it all in the preface to "Negations."'

'Negations'?'

'Yes, I gave you a copy of it.'

'Oh, yes, of course. But, did you explain, for instance, that there was no such thing as bad or good grammar?'

'N-no,' said Soames. 'Of course in art there is the good and the evil.

But in life – no.' He was rolling a cigarette. He had weak, white hands, not well washed, and with finger-tips much stained with nicotine. 'In life there are illusions of good and evil, but' – his voice trailed away to a murmur in which the words 'vieux jeu' and 'rococo' were faintly audible. I think he felt he was not doing himself justice, and feared that Rothenstein was going to point out fallacies. Anyhow, he cleared his throat and said, 'Parlons d'autre chose.'

It occurs to you that he was a fool? It didn't to me. I was young, and had not the clarity of judgment that Rothenstein already had. Soames was quite five or six years older than either of us. Also – he had written a book. It was wonderful to have written a book.

If Rothenstein had not been there, I should have revered Soames. Even as it was, I respected him. And I was very near indeed to reverence when he said he had another book coming out soon. I asked if I might ask what kind of book it was to be.

'My poems,' he answered. Rothenstein asked if this was to be the title of the book. The poet meditated on this suggestion, but said he rather thought of giving the book no title at all. 'If a book is good in itself—' he murmured, and waved his cigarette.

Rothenstein objected that absence of title might be bad for the sale of a book.

'If,' he urged, 'I went into a bookseller's and said simply, "Have you got?" or, "Have you a copy of?" how would they know what I wanted?'

'Oh, of course I should have my name on the cover,' Soames answered earnestly. 'And I rather want,' he added, looking hard at Rothenstein, 'to have a drawing of myself as frontispiece.' Rothenstein admitted that this was a capital idea, and mentioned that he was going into the country and would be there for some time. He then looked at his watch, exclaimed at the hour, paid the waiter, and went away with me to dinner. Soames remained at his post of fidelity to the glaucous witch.

'Why were you so determined not to draw him?' I asked.

'Draw him? Him? How can one draw a man who doesn't exist?'

'He is dim,' I admitted. But my mot juste fell flat. Rothenstein repeated that Soames was non-existent.

Still, Soames had written a book. I asked if Rothenstein had read 'Negations.' He said he had looked into it, 'but,' he added crisply, 'I don't profess to know anything about writing.' A reservation very characteristic of the period! Painters would not then allow that any one outside their own order had a right to any opinion about painting. This law (graven on the tablets brought down by Whistler from the summit of Fuji-yama) imposed certain limitations. If other arts than painting were not utterly unintelligible to all but the men who practiced them, the law tottered — the Monroe Doctrine, as it were, did not hold good. Therefore no painter would offer an opinion of a book without warning you at any rate that his opinion was worthless. No one is a better judge of literature than Rothenstein; but it wouldn't have done to tell him so in those days, and I knew that I must form an unaided judgment of 'Negations.'

Not to buy a book of which I had met the author face to face would have been for me in those days an impossible act of self-denial. When I returned to Oxford for the Christmas term I had duly secured 'Negations.' I used to keep it lying carelessly on the table in my room, and whenever a friend took it up and asked what it was about, I would say: 'Oh, it's rather a remarkable book. It's by a man whom I know.' Just 'what it was about' I never was able to say. Head or tail was just what I hadn't made of that slim, green volume. I found in the preface no clue to the labyrinth of contents, and in that labyrinth nothing to explain the preface.

> Lean near to life. Lean very near – nearer.
> Life is web and therein nor warp nor woof is, but web only.
> It is for this I am Catholick in church and in thought, yet do let
> swift Mood weave there what the shuttle of Mood wills.

These were the opening phrases of the preface, but those which followed were less easy to understand. Then came 'Stark: A Conte,' about a midinette who, so far as I could gather, murdered, or was about to murder, a mannequin. It was rather like a story by Catulle Mendes in which the translator had either skipped or cut out every alternate sentence. Next, a dialogue between Pan and St. Ursula, lacking, I rather thought, in 'snap.' Next, some aphorisms (entitled 'Aphorismata' [spelled in Greek]). Throughout, in fact, there was a great variety of form, and the forms had evidently been wrought with much care. It was rather the substance that eluded me. Was there, I wondered, any substance at all? It did not occur to me: suppose Enoch Soames was a fool! Up cropped a rival hypothesis: suppose *I* was! I inclined to give Soames the benefit of the doubt. I had read 'L'Après-midi d'un faune' without extracting a glimmer of meaning; yet Mallarmé, of course, was a master. How was I to know that Soames wasn't another? There was a sort of music in his prose, not indeed, arresting, but perhaps, I thought, haunting, and laden, perhaps, with meanings as deep as Mallarmé's own. I awaited his poems with an open mind.

And I looked forward to them with positive impatience after I had had a second meeting with him. This was on an evening in January. Going into the aforesaid domino-room, I had passed a table at which sat a pale man with an open book before him. He had looked from his book to me, and I looked back over my shoulder with a vague sense that I ought to have recognized him. I returned to pay my respects. After exchanging a few words, I said with a glance to the open book, 'I see I am interrupting you,' and was about to pass on, but, 'I prefer,' Soames replied in his toneless voice, 'to be interrupted,' and I obeyed his gesture that I should sit down.

I asked him if he often read here.

'Yes; things of this kind I read here,' he answered, indicating the title of his book – 'The Poems of Shelley.'

'Anything that you really' – and I was going to say 'admire?' But I cautiously left my sentence unfinished, and was glad that I had done so, for he said with unwonted emphasis, 'Anything second-rate.'

I had read little of Shelley, but, 'Of course,' I murmured, 'he's very uneven.'

'I should have thought evenness was just what was wrong with him. A deadly evenness. That's why I read him here. The noise of this place breaks the rhythm. He's tolerable here.' Soames took up the book and glanced through the pages. He laughed. Soames's laugh was a short, single, and mirthless sound from the throat, unaccompanied by any movement of the face or brightening of the eyes. 'What a period!' he uttered, laying the book down. And, 'What a country!' he added.

I asked rather nervously if he didn't think Keats had more or less held his own against the drawbacks of time and place. He admitted that there were 'passages in Keats,' but did not specify them. Of 'the older men,' as he called them, he seemed to like only Milton. 'Milton,' he said, 'wasn't sentimental.' Also, 'Milton had a dark insight.' And again, 'I can always read Milton in the reading-room.'

'The reading-room?'

'Of the British Museum. I go there every day.'

'You do? I've only been there once. I'm afraid I found it rather a depressing place. It – it seemed to sap one's vitality.'

'It does. That's why I go there. The lower one's vitality, the more sensitive one is to great art. I live near the museum. I have rooms in Dyott Street.'

'And you go round to the reading-room to read Milton?'

'Usually Milton.' He looked at me. 'It was Milton,' he certificatively added, 'who converted me to diabolism.'

'Diabolism? Oh, yes? Really?' said I, with that vague discomfort and that intense desire to be polite which one feels when a man speaks of his own religion. 'You – worship the devil?'

Soames shook his head.

'It's not exactly worship,' he qualified, sipping his absinthe. 'It's more a matter of trusting and encouraging.'

'I see, yes. I had rather gathered from the preface to "Negations" that you were a – a Catholic.'

'Je l'étais a cette époque. In fact, I still am. I am a Catholic diabolist.'

'Extreme Unction' (1893)

ERNEST DOWSON

There is a deep religious undercurrent to much of Dowson's poetry; shortly before his death he converted to Catholicism.

Upon the eyes, the lips, the feet,
On all the passages of sense,
The atoning oil is spread with sweet
Renewal of lost innocence.

The feet, that lately ran so fast
To meet desire, are soothly sealed;
The eyes, that were so often cast
On vanity, are touched and healed.

From troublous sights and sounds set free;
In such a twilight hour of breath,
Shall one retrace his life, or see,
Through shadows, the true face of death?

Vials of mercy! Sacring oils!
I know not where nor when I come,
Nor through what wanderings and toils,
To crave of you Viaticum.

Yet, when the walls of flesh grow weak,
In such an hour, it well may be,
Through mist and darkness, light will break,
And each anointed sense will see.

Extract from 'Rosa Alchemica' (1896)

W. B. YEATS

One of Yeats's earliest published short stories, this reveals much about his own esoteric interests, and clearly links a decadent sensibility with a sensuous religiosity. Compare the protagonist's description of his study and his leather-bound books with Des Esseinte's description of his house in À Rebours.

O blessed and happy he, who knowing the mysteries of the gods, sanctifies his life, and purifies his soul, celebrating orgies in the mountains with holy purifications. – *Euripides.*

I

A few years ago an extraordinary religious frenzy took hold upon the peasantry of a remote Connemara headland; and a number of eccentric men and women, who had turned an old customhouse into a kind of college, were surprised at prayer, as it was then believed, by a mob of fishermen, stone masons, and small farmers, and beaten to death with stones, which were heaped up close at hand to be ready for the next breach in the wave-battered pier. Vague rumours of pagan ceremonies and mysterious idolatries had for some time drifted among the cabins; and the indignation of the ignorant had been further inflamed by a priest, unfrocked for drunkenness, who had preached by the road-side of the secret coming of the Anti-Christ. I first heard of these unfortunates, on whom the passion for universal ideas, which distinguishes the Celtic and Latin races, was to bring so dreadful a martyrdom, but a few weeks before the end; and the change in my opinions which has made my writings so much less popular and intelligible, and driven me to the verge of taking the habit of St. Dominic, was brought about by the strange experiences I endured in their presence.

I had just published *Rosa Alchemica*, a little work on the Alchemists, somewhat in the manner of Sir Thomas Browne, and had received many letters from believers in the arcane sciences, upbraiding what they called my timidity, for they could not believe so evident sympathy but the sympathy of the artist, which is half pity, for everything which has moved men's hearts in any age. I had discovered, early in my researches, that their doctrine was no merely chemical phantasy, but a philosophy they applied to the world, to the elements and to man himself; and that they sought to fashion gold out of common metals merely as part of an universal transmutation of all things into some divine and imperishable substance; and this enabled me to make my little book a fanciful reverie over the transmutation of life into art, and a cry of measureless desire for a world made wholly of essences.

I was sitting dreaming of what I had written, in my house in one of the old parts of Dublin; a house my ancestors had made almost famous through their part in the politics of the city and their friendships with the famous men of their generations; and was feeling an unwonted happiness at having at last accomplished a long-cherished design, and made my rooms an expression of this favourite doctrine. The portraits, of more historical than artistic interest, had gone; and tapestry, full of the blue and bronze of peacocks, fell over the doors, and shut out all history and activity untouched with beauty and peace; and now when I looked at my Crivelli and pondered on the rose in the hand of the Virgin, wherein the form was so delicate and precise that it seemed more like a thought than a flower, or at the grey dawn and rapturous faces of my Francesca, I knew all a Christian's ecstasy without his slavery to rule and custom; when I pondered over the antique bronze gods and goddesses, which I had mortgaged my house to buy, I had all a pagan's delight in various beauty and without his terror at sleepless destiny and his labour with many sacrifices; and I had only to go to my bookshelf, where every book was bound in leather, stamped with intricate ornament, and of a carefully chosen colour: Shakespeare in the orange of the glory of the world, Dante in the dull red of his anger, Milton in the blue grey of his formal calm; and I could experience what I would of human passions without their bitterness and without satiety. I had gathered about me all gods because I believed in none, and experienced every pleasure because I gave myself to none, but held myself apart, individual, indissoluble, a mirror of polished steel: I looked in the triumph of this imagination at the birds of Hera, glowing in the firelight as though they were wrought of jewels; and to my mind, for which symbolism was a necessity, they seemed the doorkeepers of my world, shutting out all that was not of as affluent a beauty as their own; and for a moment I thought as I had thought in so many other moments, that it was possible to rob life of every bitterness except the bitterness of death; and then a thought which had followed this thought, time after time, filled me with a passionate sorrow. All those forms: that Madonna with her brooding purity, those rapturous faces singing in the morning light, those bronze divinities with their passionless dignity, those wild shapes rushing from despair to despair, belonged to a divine world wherein I had no part; and every experience, however profound, every perception, however exquisite, would bring me the bitter dream of a limitless energy I could never know, and even in my most perfect moment I would be two selves, the one watching with heavy eyes the other's moment of content. I had heaped about me the gold born in the crucibles of others; but the supreme dream of the alchemist, the transmutation of the weary heart into a weariless spirit, was as far from me as, I doubted not, it had been from him also. I turned to my last purchase, a set of alchemical apparatus which, the dealer in the Rue le Peletier had assured me, once belonged to Raymond Lully, and as I joined the *alembic* to the *athanor* and laid the *lavacrum maris* at their side, I understood the alchemical doctrine, that all beings, divided from the great deep where spirits wander, one and yet a multitude, are weary; and sympathized, in the pride of my connoisseurship, with the consuming thirst for destruction which made the alchemist veil under his symbols of lions and dragons, of eagles and ravens, of dew and of nitre, a search for an essence which would dissolve all mortal things. I repeated to myself the ninth key of Basilius Valentinus, in which he compares the fire of the last day to the fire of the alchemist, and the world to the alchemist's furnace, and would have us know that all must be dissolved before the divine substance, material gold or immaterial ecstasy, awake. I had dissolved indeed the mortal world and lived amid immortal essences, but had obtained no miraculous ecstasy. As I thought of these things, I drew aside

the curtains and looked out into the darkness, and it seemed to my troubled fancy that all those little points of light filling the sky were the furnaces of innumerable divine alchemists, who labour continually, turning lead into gold, weariness into ecstasy, bodies into souls, the darkness into God; and at their perfect labour my mortality grew heavy, and I cried out, as so many dreamers and men of letters in our age have cried, for the birth of that elaborate spiritual beauty which could alone uplift souls weighted with so many dreams.

II

My reverie was broken by a loud knocking at the door, and I wondered the more at this because I had no visitors, and had bid my servants do all things silently, lest they broke the dream of my inner life. Feeling a little curious, I resolved to go to the door myself, and, taking one of the silver candlesticks from the mantlepiece, began to descend the stairs. The servants appeared to be out, for though the sound poured through every corner and crevice of the house there was no stir in the lower rooms. I remembered that because my needs were so few, my part in life so little, they had begun to come and go as they would, often leaving me alone for hours. The emptiness and silence of a world from which I had driven everything but dreams suddenly overwhelmed me, and I shuddered as I drew the bolt. I found before me Michael Robartes, whom I had not seen for years, and whose wild red hair, fierce eyes, sensitive, tremulous lips and rough clothes, made him look now, just as they used to do fifteen years before, something between a debauchee, a saint, and a peasant. He had recently come to Ireland, he said, and wished to see me on a matter of importance: indeed, the only matter of importance for him and for me. His voice brought up before me our student years in Paris, and remembering the magnetic power he had once possessed over me, a little fear mingled with much annoyance at this irrelevant intrusion, as I led the way up the wide staircase, where Swift had passed joking and railing, and Curran telling stories and quoting Greek, in simpler days, before men's minds, subtilized and complicated by the romantic movement in art and literature, began to tremble on the verge of some unimagined revelation. I felt that my hand shook, and saw that the light of the candle wavered and quivered more than it need have upon the Maenads on the old French panels, making them look like the first beings slowly shaping in the formless and void darkness. When the door had closed, and the peacock curtain, glimmering like many-coloured flame, fell between us and the world, I felt, in a way I could not understand, that some singular and unexpected thing was about to happen. I went over to the mantlepiece, and finding that a little chainless bronze censer, set, upon the outside, with pieces of painted china by Orazio Fontana, which I had filled with antique amulets, had fallen upon its side and poured out its contents, I began to gather the amulets into the bowl, partly to collect my thoughts and partly with that habitual reverence which seemed to me the due of things so long connected with secret hopes and fears. 'I see,' said Michael Robartes, 'that you are still fond of incense, and I can show you an incense more precious than any you have ever seen,' and as he spoke he took the censer out of my hand and put the amulets in a little heap between the *athanor* and the *alembic*. I sat down, and he sat down at the side of the fire, and sat there for awhile looking into the fire, and holding the censer in his hand. 'I have come to ask you something,' he said, 'and the incense will fill the room, and our thoughts, with its sweet odour while we are talking. I got it from an old man in Syria, who said it was made from flowers, of one kind with the flowers that laid their heavy purple petals upon the hands and upon the hair and upon the feet of Christ in the Garden of Gethsemane, and folded Him in their heavy breath, until he cried against the cross and his destiny.' He shook some dust into the censer out of a small silk bag, and set the censer upon the floor and lit the dust which sent up a blue stream of smoke, that spread out over the ceiling, and flowed downwards again until it was like Milton's banyan tree. It filled me, as incense often does, with a faint sleepiness, so that I started when he said, 'I have come to ask you that question which I asked you in Paris, and which you left Paris rather than answer.'

He had turned his eyes towards me, and I saw them glitter in the firelight, and through the incense, as I replied: 'You mean, will I become an initiate of your Order of the Alchemical Rose? I would not consent in

Paris, when I was full of unsatisfied desire, and now that I have at last fashioned my life according to my desire, am I likely to consent?'

'You have changed greatly since then,' he answered. 'I have read your books, and now I see you among all these images, and I understand you better than you do yourself, for I have been with many and many dreamers at the same cross-ways. You have shut away the world and gathered the gods about you, and if you do not throw yourself at their feet, you will be always full of lassitude, and of wavering purpose, for a man must forget he is miserable in the bustle and noise of the multitude in this world and in time; or seek a mystical union with the multitude who govern this world and time.' And then he murmured something I could not hear, and as though to someone I could not see.

For a moment the room appeared to darken, as it used to do when he was about to perform some singular experiment, and in the darkness the peacocks upon the doors seemed to glow with a more intense colour. I cast off the illusion, which was, I believe, merely caused by memory, and by the twilight of incense, for I would not acknowledge that he could overcome my now mature intellect; and I said: 'Even if I grant that I need a spiritual belief and some form of worship, why should I go to Eleusis and not to Calvary?' He leaned forward and began speaking with a slightly rhythmical intonation, and as he spoke I had to struggle again with the shadow, as of some older night than the night of the sun, which began to dim the light of the candles and to blot out the little gleams upon the corner of picture-frames and on the bronze divinities, and to turn the blue of the incense to a heavy purple; while it left the peacocks to glimmer and glow as though each separate colour were a living spirit. I had fallen into a profound dream-like reverie in which I heard him speaking as at a distance. 'And yet there is no one who communes with only one god,' he was saying, 'and the more a man lives in imagination and in a refined understanding, the more gods does he meet with and talk with, and the more does he come under the power of Roland, who sounded in the Valley of Roncesvalles the last trumpet of the body's will and pleasure; and of Hamlet, who saw them perishing away, and sighed; and of Faust, who looked for them up and down the world and could not find them; and under the power of all those countless divinities who have taken upon themselves spiritual bodies in the minds of the modern poets and romance writers, and under the power of the old divinities, who since the Renaissance have won everything of their ancient worship except the sacrifice of birds and fishes, the fragrance of garlands and the smoke of incense. The many think humanity made these divinities, and that it can unmake them again; but we who have seen them pass in rattling harness, and in soft robes, and heard them speak with articulate voices while we lay in deathlike trance, know that they are always making and unmaking humanity, which is indeed but the trembling of their lips.'

He had stood up and begun to walk to and fro, and had become in my waking dream a shuttle weaving an immense purple web whose folds had begun to fill the room. The room seemed to have become inexplicably silent, as though all but the web and the weaving were at an end in the world. 'They have come to us; they have come to us,' the voice began again; 'all that have ever been in your reverie, all that you have met with in books. There is Lear, his head still wet with the thunder-storm, and he laughs because you thought yourself an existence who are but a shadow, and him a shadow who is an eternal god; and there is Beatrice, with her lips half parted in a smile, as though all the stars were about to pass away in a sigh of love; and there is the mother of the God of humility who cast so great a spell over men that they have tried to unpeople their hearts that he might reign alone, but she holds in her hand the rose whose every petal is a god; and there, O swiftly she comes! is Aphrodite under a twilight falling from the wings of numberless sparrows, and about her feet are the grey and white doves.' In the midst of my dream I saw him hold out his left arm and pass his right hand over it as though he stroked the wings of doves. I made a violent effort which seemed almost to tear me in two, and said with forced determination: 'You would sweep me away into an indefinite world which fills me with terror; and yet a man is a great man just in so far as he can make his mind reflect everything with indifferent precision like a mirror.' I seemed to be perfectly master of myself, and went on, but more rapidly: 'I command you to leave me at once, for your ideas and phantasies are but the illusions that creep like maggots into civilizations when they begin to decline, and into minds when they begin to decay.' I had grown suddenly angry, and seizing the *alembic* from the table, was about to rise and strike him with it, when the peacocks on the door behind him appeared to grow immense; and then the *alembic* fell from my fingers and I was drowned in a tide of green and blue and bronze feathers, and as I struggled hopelessly I heard a distant voice saying: 'Our master Avicenna has written that all life proceeds out of corruption.' The glittering feathers had now covered me completely, and I knew that I had struggled for hundreds of years, and was conquered at last. I was sinking into the depth when the green and blue and bronze that seemed to fill the world became a sea of flame and swept me away, and as I was swirled along I heard a voice over my head cry, 'The mirror is broken in two pieces,' and another voice answer, 'The mirror is broken in four pieces,' and a more distant voice cry with an exultant cry, 'The mirror is broken into numberless pieces'; and then a multitude of pale hands were reaching towards me, and strange gentle faces bending above me, and half wailing and half caressing voices uttering words that were forgotten the moment they were spoken. I was being lifted out of the tide of flame, and felt my memories, my hopes, my thoughts, my will, everything I held to be myself, melting away; then I seemed to rise through numberless companies of beings who were, I understood, in some way more certain than thought, each wrapped in his eternal moment, in the perfect lifting of an arm, in a little circlet of rhythmical words, in dreaming with dim eyes and half-closed eyelids. And then I passed beyond these forms, which were so beautiful they had almost ceased to be, and, having endured strange moods, melancholy, as it seemed, with the weight of many worlds, I passed into that Death which is Beauty herself, and into that Loneliness which all the multitudes desire without ceasing. All things that had ever lived seemed to come and dwell in my heart, and I in theirs; and I had never again known mortality or tears, had I not suddenly fallen from the certainty of vision into the uncertainty of dream, and become a drop of molten gold falling with immense rapidity, through a night elaborate with stars, and all about me a melancholy exultant wailing. I fell and fell and fell, and then the wailing was but the wailing of the wind in the chimney, and I awoke to find myself leaning upon the table and supporting my head with my hands. I saw the *alembic* swaying from side to side in the distant corner it had rolled to, and Michael Robartes watching me and waiting. 'I will go wherever you will,' I said, 'and do whatever you bid me, for I have been with eternal things.' 'I knew,' he replied, 'you must need answer as you have answered, when I heard the storm begin. You must come to a great distance, for we were commanded to build our temple between the pure multitude by the waves and the impure multitude of men.'

'The Tables of the Law' (1896)

W. B. YEATS

The Tables of the Law, also published in the Savoy, *sees Yeats explore the appeal of heresy and the danger of obsession.*

I

'Will you permit me, Aherne,' I said, 'to ask you a question which I have wanted to ask you for years; and have not asked because we have grown nearly strangers. Why did you refuse the cassock and the berretta, and almost at the last moment? I never expected you, of all men, to become "a spoilt priest." When you and I lived together, you cared neither for wine, women, nor money, and were absorbed in the theological and mystical studies.' I had watched through dinner for a moment to put my question, and ventured now, because he had thrown off a little of the reserve and indifference, which, ever since his last return to Italy, had taken the place of out once close friendship. He had just questioned me too, about certain private and almost sacred things, and my frankness had earned, I thought, a like frankness from him.

When I began to speak he was lifting to his lips a glass of that old wine which he could choose so well and valued so little; and while I spoke, he set it slowly and meditatively upon the table and held it there, its deep red light dyeing his long delicate fingers. The impression of his face and form, as they were then, is still vivid with me, and is inseparable from another and fanciful impression: the impression of a man holding a flame in his naked hand. He was to me, at that moment, the supreme type of our race, which when it has risen above, or is sunken below, the formalisms of half-education and the rationalisms of conventional affirmation and denial, turns away from practicable desires and intuitions, towards desires to unbounded that no human vessel can contain them, intuitions so immaterial that their sudden and far-off fire leaves heavy darkness about

hand and foot. He had the nature, which is half alchemist, half soldier of
fortune, and must needs turn action into dreaming, and dreaming into
action; and for such there is no order, no finality, no contentment in this
world. At the Jesuit school in Paris he had made one of the little group,
which used to gather in corners of the playing field, or in remote class
rooms, to hear the speculative essays which we wrote and read in secret.
More orthodox in most of his beliefs than Michael Robartes, he had
surpassed him in a fanciful hatred of all life, and this hatred had found
expression in the curious paradox, half borrowed from some fanatical
monk, half invented by himself; that the beautiful arts were sent into the
world to overthrow nations, and finally life herself, by sowing everywhere
unlimited desires, like torches thrown into a burning city. This idea was
not at the time, I believe, more than a paradox, a plume of the pride of
youth; and it was only after his leaving school that he endured the
fermentation of belief which is coming upon our people with the
reawakening of their imaginative life.

Presently he stood up, saying:

'Come, and I will show you, for you at any rate will understand,' and
taking candles from the table, he lit the way into a long paved passage that
led to his private chapel. We passed between the portraits of the Jesuits
and priests, some of no little fame, whom his family had given to the
Church; and framed photographs of the pictures which had especially
moved him and the few painting his small fortune, eked out by an almost
penurious abstinence from the things most men desire, had enabled him to
buy in his travels. The photographs of pictures were from the masterpieces
of many schools: but in all, the beauty, whether it was a beauty of religion,
of love, or of some fantastical vision of mountain and wood, was the beauty
achieved by temperaments which seek always an absolute of emotions,
and have their most continual, though not most perfect expression, in the
legends and music and vigils of the Celtic peoples. The certitude of a fierce
or gracious fervour in the enraptured faces of the Francesca's, and Crivelli's
Madonnas and in the august faces of the sibyls of Michael Angelo; and the
incertitude, as of souls trembling between the excitement of the spirit and
the excitement of the flesh, in the wavering faces Sodoma made for the

churches of Siena, and in the faces like thin flames, imagined by the modern symbolists and pre-Raphaelites, had often made that long, gray, dim, echoing passage seem to me like a vestibule of eternity.

Almost every detail of the chapel, which we entered by a narrow Gothic door, whose threshold had been worn smooth by the secret worshippers of the penal times, was vivid in my memory; for it was in this chapel that I had first, when but a boy, been moved by the medievalism which is now, I think, the governing influence on my life. The only thing that seemed new was a square bronze box; like those made in ancient times of more precious substances to hold the sacred books; which stood before the six unlighted candles and the ebony crucifix upon the alter. Aherne made me sit down on a long oaken bench, and having bowed very low before the crucifix, took the bronze box from the altar, and sat down beside me with the box upon his knees.

'You will perhaps have forgotten,' he said, 'most of what you have read about Joachim of Flora, for he is little more than a name to even the best read. He was an abbot in Corace in the twelfth century, and is best known for his prophecy, in a book called *Expositio in Apocalypsin*, that the Kingdom of the Father was passed, the Kingdom of the Son passing, the Kingdom of the Spirit yet to come. The Kingdom of the Spirit was to be a complete triumph of the Spirit, the *spiritualis intelligentia* he called it, over the dead letter. He had many followers among the more extreme Franciscans, and these were accused of possessing a secret book of his called the *Liber Inducens in Evangelium Aeternum*. Again and again groups of visionaries were accused of possessing this terrible book, in which the freedom of the Renaissance lay hidden, until at last Pope Alexander IV had it found and cast into the flames. I have here the greatest treasure the world contains. I have a copy of that book, and see what great artists have made the robes in which is is wrapped. This bronze box was made by Benvenuto Cellini, who covered it with gods and demons, whose eyes are closed to signify absorption in the inner light.' He lifted the lid and took out a book bound in old leather, covered with filigree work of tarnished silver. 'And this cover bound for Canevari; while Giulio Clovio, the one artist of the later Renaissance who could give to his work the beauty of a hidden hope, tore out the beginning page of every chapter of the old copy and set in its place a page, surmounted by an elaborate letter, and a miniature of some on of the great whose example was cited in the chapter; and wherever the writing left a little space elsewhere, he put some delicate emblem or intricate pattern.'

I took the book in my hands and began turning over the jewel-like pages, holding it close to the candle to discover the texture of the paper.

'Where did you get this amazing book?' I said. 'If genuine, and I cannot judge by this light, you have discovered one of the most precious things in the world.'

'It is certainly genuine,' he replied. 'When the original was destroyed, one copy alone remained, and was in the hands of a lute player of Florence, and from him it passed to his son, and so from generation to generation, until it came to a lute player, who was father to Benvenuto Cellini, and from his it passed to Giulio Clovio, and from Giulio Clovio to a Roman engraver; and then from generation to generation, the story of its wandering passing on with it, until it came into possession of the family of Aretino, and so to Giulio Aretino, an artist and worker in metals, and student of the kabalistic heresies of Pico della Mirandola. He spent many nights with me at Rome discussing philosophy; and at last I won his confidence so perfectly that he showed me this, his greatest treasure; and, finding how much I valued it, and feeling that he himself was growing old and beyond the help of its mysterious teaching, he sold it to me for no great sum, considering its great preciousness.'

'What is the doctrine?' I said. 'Some medieval straw-splitting about the nature of the Trinity, which is only useful to-day to show how many things are unimportant to us, which once shook the world?'

'I could never make you understand,' he said with a deep sigh, 'that nothing is unimportant in belief, but even you will admit that this book goes to the heard. Do you see the tables on which the commandments were written in Latin?' I looked to the end of the room opposite the altar, and saw that the two marble tablets were gone, and two large empty tablets of ivory, like large copies of the little tablets we set over out desks, had taken their place. 'It has swept the commandments of the Father away,' he went

on, 'and displaced the commandments of the Son by the commandments of the Holy Spirit. The first book is called *Fractura Tabularum*. In the first chapter it mentions the names of the great artists who made them graven things and the likeness of many things, and adored them and served them; and in the second the names of the great wits who took the name of the Lord their God in vain; and that long third chapter, set with the emblems of sanctified faces, and having wings upon its borders, is the praise of breakers of the seventh day and wasters of the six days. Those two chapters tell of men and women who railed upon their parents, remembering that their god was older than the god of their parents; and that, which has the sword of Michael for an emblem, commends the kinds that wrought secret murder and so won for the people a peace that was *amore somnoque gravata et vestibus versicoloribus*, "heavy with love and sleep and many-coloured raiment;" and that with the pale star at the closing has the lives of the noble youths who loved the wives of others and were transformed into memories, which have transformed many poorer hearts into sweet flames; and that with the winged head is the history of the robbers, who lived, upon the sea or in the desert, lives which it compares to the twittering of the string of a bow, *nervi stridentis instar*; and those two last, that are fire and gold, are devoted to the satirists who bore false witness against their neighbours and yet illustrated eternal wrath; and to those that have coveted more than other men the house of God, and all things that are his, which no man has seen and handled, except in madness and in dreaming.

'The second book, which is called *Straminis Deflagratio*, recounts the conversations Joachim of Flora held in his monastery at Corace, and afterwards in his monastery in the mountains of Sylae, with travellers and pilgrims, upon the laws of many countries; how chastity was a virtue and robbery a little thing in such a land, and robbery a crime and unchastity a little thing in such a land; and of persons who had flung themselves upon laws and become *decussa veste dei sidera*, 'stars shaken out of the raiment of God.'

'The third book, which is the finish, is called *Lex Secreta*, and describes the true inspiration of action, the only Eternal Evangel; and ends with a vision, which he saw among the mountains of Sylae, of his disciples sitting throned in the blue deep of the air and laughing aloud, with a laughter which it compares to the rustling of the wings of Time.'

'I know little of Joachim of Flora,' I said, 'except that Dante set him in Paradise among the great doctors. If he held a heresy so singular, I cannot understand how no rumours of it came to the ears of Dante; and Dante made no peace with the enemies of the Church.'

'Joachim of Flora acknowledged openly the authority of the Church, and even asked that all his published writings, and those to be published by his desire after his death, should be submitted to the censorship of the Pope. He considered that those, whose work was to live and not to reveal, were children and that the Pope was their father; and he taught in secret that certain others, and in always increasing numbers, were elected, not for life's sake, but to reveal that hidden substance of God which is colour and music and softness and sweet odour; and that these have no father but the Holy Spirit. Just as poets and painters and musicians labour at their works, building them with flawless and lawful things alike so long as they embody the beauty that is beyond the grave; these children of the Holy Spirit labour at their moments with eyes upon the shining substance on which Time has heaped the refuse of creation; for the world only exists to be a tale in the ears of coming generations; and terror and content, birth and death, love and hatred and the fruit of the Tree are but instruments for that supreme art which is to win us from life and gather us into eternity like doves into their dove-cots.

'I shall go away in a little while and travel into many lands, that I may know all accidents and destinies, and when I return, will write my secret law upon those ivory tablets, just as poets and romance writers have written the principles of their art in prefaces; and will gather pupils about me that they may discover their law in the study of my law, and the Kingdom of the Holy Spirit be more widely and firmly established.'

He was pacing up and down, and I listened to the fervour of his words and watched the excitement of his gestures with not a little concern. I had been accustomed to welcome the most singular speculations, and had always found them as harmless as the Persian cat, who half closes her meditative eyes and stretches out her long claws, before my fire. But not I longed to battle in the interests of orthodoxy, even of the commonplace: and yet could find nothing better to say than:

'It is not necessary to judge everyone by the law, for we have also Christ's commandment of love.'

He turned and said, looking at me with shining eyes:

'Jonathan Swift made a soul for the gentlemen of this city by hating his neighbour as himself.'

'At any rate, you cannot deny that to teach so dangerous a doctrine is to accept a terrible responsibility.'

'Leonardo da Vinci,' he replied, 'has this noble sentence, "The hope and desire of returning home to one's former state, is like the moth's desire for the light; and the man, who with constant longing awaits each new month and new year — deeming that the things he longs for are ever too late in coming — does not perceive that he is longing for his own destruction." How then can the pathway which will lead us into the heart of God be other than dangerous? Why should you, who are no materialist, cherish the continuity and order of the world as those do who have only the world? You do not value the writers who will express nothing unless their reason

understands how it will make what is called the right more easy; why then will you deny a like freedom to the supreme art, the art which is the foundation of all arts? Yes, I shall send out of this chapel saints, lovers, rebels, and prophets: souls which will surround themselves with peace, as with a nest made of grass; and perhaps others over whom I shall weep. The dust shall fall for many years over this little box; and then I shall open it; and the tumults, which are, perhaps, the flames of the last day, shall come from under the lid.'

I did not reason with him that night, because his excitement was great and I feared to make him angry; and when I called at his house a few days later, he was gone and his house was locked up and empty. I have deeply regretted my failure both to combat his heresy and to test the genuineness of his strange book. Since my conversion I have indeed done penance for an error which I was only able to measure after some years.

II

I was walking along one of the Dublin quays, about ten years after our conversation, stopping from time to time to turn over the books upon an old bookstall, and thinking, curiously enough of the destinies of the little group of fellow students who had shared so many speculations at the school in Paris, and particularly of the terrible destiny of Michael Robartes and his disciples, when I saw a tall, bent man walking slowly in front of me. He stopped presently at a little shop, in the window of which were blue and white statues of the Virgin, and gilded statues of St. Patrick and his crosier. His face was now half turned towards me, and I recognized in the lifeless mask with dim eyes what have been the resolute, delicate face of Owen Aherne. I walked towards him, but had not gone many yards before he turned away, as though he had seen me, and went hastily down a side street.

During the next few weeks I enquired of all who had once known him, but he had made himself known to no one, and knocked without result at the door of his old house. I had nearly persuaded myself that I was mistaken, when I saw him again, and this time in a back street behind Four Courts, and followed him until he stopped at the door of his house.

I laid my hand upon his arm; he turned around, and quite without surprise; and, indeed, it is possible that to him, whose inner life had soaked up the outer life, a parting of many years was a parting from forenoon to afternoon. He stood holding the door half open, as though he would keep me from entering, and would, perhaps, have parted from me with no further words had I not said:

'Aherne, you trusted me once, will you not trust me again, and tell me what has come of the ideas we discussed ten years ago? But perhaps you have long forgotten them.'

'You have a right to hear,' he answered; 'for having told you the ideas, it is necessary that I tell you the danger they contain; but when you have heard, we part for good and all: I must be hidden away, for I am lost.'

I followed him through the paved passage, and saw that its corners were choked with dust and cobwebs; and that the pictures were shrouded with cobwebs and gray with dust; and, when he opened the door of the chapel, I saw that the dust and cobwebs which covered the ruby and sapphire saints in the window had made it very dim. He sat down wearily, not seeming to notice whether I was standing or sitting, and pointed to where the ivory tablets glimmered faintly in the deep gloom. I saw that they were covered with very small writing, and went up to them and began to read them. The writing was an elaborate casuistry, illustrated apparently with many examples, but whether from his own life, or from the life of others, I do not know. Before I had done more than read a sentence here and there, I turned from them, for Aherne had begun to speak in a low monotonous voice.

'I am outside the salvation of Him who died for sinners, because I have lost the power of committing a sin. I found the secret law of my life, and, finding it, no longer desired to transgress, because it was my own law. Whatever my intellect and my soul commanded, I did, and sin passed from me, and I ceased to be among those for whom Christ died.' And at the name of Christ he crossed himself with the involuntary gesture which marks those who have crossed themselves from childhood. 'At first I tried to sin by breaking my law, although without desire; but the sin without desire is shadow, like the sins of some phantom one has not visited even in dreams. You who are not lost, who may still speak to men and women, tell them that it is necessary to make an arbitrary law that one may be among those for whom Christ died.'

I went over and stood beside him and said:

'Prayer and penance will make you like other men.'

'Not,' he replied, 'unless they can take from my knowledge of the secret law.'

I used some argument, which has passed out of my memory, but his strong intellect, which seemed all the stronger and more active from contrast with the weary monotony of his voice, tore my argument to pieces. I had gone on to heap argument on argument, had he not risen and led me from the chapel, repeating, 'We part for good and all; for I must be hidden away.'

I followed, intending to come to him again the next day; but as I stood on the door of the house a sudden hope came to my mind, and I said:

'Will you lend me the *Liber Inducens in Evangelium Aeternum* for a few days, that I may have it examined by an expert?'

'I have burned the book and flung the box into the sea.'

When I came the next day with a Jesuit Father from the College of St. Francis Xavier, the house was locked up and apparently empty once more.

'The Three Witches' (1896)

ERNEST DOWSON

This poem is full of imagery evocative of magic and witchcraft,
but it is also tinged with death and melancholy. The lines suggest
the decadents share a kinship with the witches who 'wander
through the meaning of a day and see no light'.

All the moon-shed nights are over,
    And the days of gray and dun;
There is neither may nor clover,
    And the day and night are one.

Not an hamlet, not a city
    Meets our strained and tearless eyes;
In the plain without a pity,
    Where the wan grass droops and dies.

We shall wander through the meaning
    Of a day and see no light,
For our lichened arms are leaning
    On the ends of endless night.

We, the children of Astarte,
    Dear abortions of the moon,
In a gay and silent party,
    We are riding to you soon.

Burning ramparts, ever burning!
 To the flame which never dies
We are yearning, yearning, yearning,
 With our gay and tearless eyes.

In the plain without a pity,
 (Not an hamlet, not a city)
 Where the wan grass droops and dies.

'It Was Deep April' (1893)

MICHAEL FIELD

'Michael Field' was the pseudonym adopted by Katherine Bradley (1846–1914) and her niece and ward Edith Cooper (1862–1913). The two became lovers, and spent their lives devoted to each other and to writing. Their spiritual journey was typically decadent: they were atheist aesthetes, then practising pagans, then converted to Roman Catholicism in their final years. 'It Was Deep April' touches on eroticism, classical paganism and rebellion as they pledge to live as 'Poets and lovers evermore'.

It was deep April, and the morn
   Shakespere was born;
The world was on us, pressing sore;
My love and I took hands and swore,
   Against the world, to be
Poets and lovers evermore,
To laugh and dream on Lethe's shore,
To sing to Charon in his boat,
Heartening the timid souls afloat;
Of judgement never to take heed,
But to those fast-locked souls to speed,
Whoe never from Apollo fled,
Who spent no hour among the dead;
   Continually
   With them to dwell,
Indifferent to heaven and hell.

5

Et In Arcadia Ego
– DEATH

They are not long, the days of wine and roses.
Ernest Dowson

'On the Kind of Fiction Called Morbid' (1896)

VINCENT O'SULLIVAN

'Morbid' was an especially loaded term in the 1890s, being both a byword for decadent and a euphemism for homosexuality. The Decadent movement was seen by many as a kind of sickness, and any fiction concerned with death, illness or other aberration from standard morality was treated as a dangerous growth that needed to be excised from the culture. O'Sullivan's essay is a mature and interesting response to the term.

'This is a poison-bad world for the romancer, this Anglo-Saxon world,' wrote Robert Louis Stevenson to Mr. Sidney Colvin: and if a popular writer with an obvious style, after his years of experience, came to this conclusion, we risk little in asserting that the same conclusion has been reached by many another writer whose style is not obvious, and who is not so popular. Amongst these, the man who would be always introducing the thin presence of Death is, without doubt, the most reviled; we will have nothing of a fellow who comes to our feasts with a skull. And though we all agree that *Memento homo quia pulvis es* is a fine and wise saying, yet, i' faith! we are content to leave it at that; and we clap the rogue who recalls it in the stocks. Nay! Ash Wednesday would have been long ago rubbed out of the calendar, save that we are careful not to understand the full significance of it; just as we are careful not to understand the full significance of Good Friday.

The smiling gentleman who hails us in the street does not like to think that one day he must be dead; archbishops are supposed not to like a dwelling on that; and a certain parson of easy life, whose business it is to preach mortality, when invited by a plain writer to fall into a better acquaintance with the cold guide who shall lead him to the Eternal Hills, flies into a passion, calls my plain writer (of all things in the world!)

immoral, and sits down, raging, to write insolent letters to the papers. But (you will ask), do not these people give a man the credit of his courage in facing what they dare not face? Well, no. For when a man has done the day's appointed labour, he stirs the fire, sinks into his armchair, and lo! in a trice he spurns the hearth and is off swinging the sword and aiding somewhat sulky damsels with De Marsac; or, if he is of a cold habit of body, he wanders in lanes where the clover breathes, and John and Joan while away the white-winged hours a-wooing. Or again, he hies to the ball, and watches the tenderness with which my lord and the farmer's daughter take the floor. If, then, to this man a person of wry visage and hearse-like airs comes offering a sombre story – why, up he leaps, grasps the intrusive fellow by the shoulders, and lands him in the street. No; it is certain that abnormal nerves are not understood or thought proper in the suburban villa: and they are not tolerated by the Press, which is almost the same thing. Even editors, those cocks that show how the popular wind blows, if they have no kicks, have few ha'pence for the writer of stories which are not sops to our pleasure. The thought of death is not pleasant! (folk may be imagined to exclaim); to escape that we laugh at sorry farces and the works of Mr. Mark Twain; and yet, here is a zany with a hatful of dun thoughts formed to make one meditate on one's tomb for a week! Still, for him, poor devil! life is not all (as they say) beer and skittles. With an impatience of facility, he sets to work sedulously on a branch of art which he is pleased to consider difficult; it cannot be pleasant work, since it progresses with shudders and cold sweats; it cannot be easy, since it is acknowledged to be no easy thing to turn the blood from men's faces. He is even charmed by the fancy that he is driving his pen to a very high measure. He may (by chance) be right; he is possibly wrong; but I am glad to say I have yet to hear that Banquo's ghost at the feast, and Cæsar's ghost in the tent, are deemed infamous, or (as the cant goes) immoral. And, talking of Shakespeare, has it ever occurred to you how the critics would waggle their heads at 'Romeo and Juliet,' if it were presented to-day as a new piece by William Shakespeare, Esq.?

'As in a vault, an ancient receptacle,
Where, for these many hundred years, the bones
Of all my buried ancestors are pack'd;
Where bloody Tybalt, yet but green in earth,
Lies festering in his shroud; where, as they say,
At some hours in the night spirits resort; –
Alack! alack! is it not like, that I,
So early waking, – what with loathsome smells,
And shrieks like mandrakes' torn out of the earth,
That living mortals, hearing them, run mad; –
O, if I wake, shall I not be distraught,
Environed with all these hideous fears?
And madly play with my forefathers' joints?
And pluck the mangled Tybalt from his shroud?
And, in this rage, with some great kinsman's bone,
As with a club, dash out my desperate brains?'

Methinks I see the words: 'exotic,' 'morbid,' 'unhealthy,' ready-made
for that! Ah! how, then, can my modern writer expect to be suffered, any
more than we suffer an undertaker to send out cards setting forth the
excellence of his wares. When he takes to the road, he must know that he
is in for a weary and footsore journey: comely persons, in beautiful
garments, with eyes full of invitation look down from bordering windows
and jeer at his sober parade; he sees cool, shaded by-lanes which are never
for him; others pass him on the road singing blithe, gamesome songs, and
he is left to loiter. And be sure he travels in glum company: the stiff-
featured dead, with their thin hands and strange smile, fall into step with
him and tell him their dream-like tales. The poor dead, whom we all forget
so soon on this sunny earth! I think they tell him that they have a kindness
for those who perform the last offices for them: the dead villager for the
barber and the crone, the dead peer for the undertakers who come by night
to Belgrave Square. Perhaps it is from fear of the ghosts who attend the
march, that the writers of aweful stories are few and far between, up and
down the world. And when we meet with such a one, whose head is humming

like a top from the gray talk of his fellow-passengers, should we not thank (rather than stone) him for his sense of the decency of things, which prevents him from going tearing mad and holding the highway with a gun? I will wager that the recognition of this is all he asks of reward from the 'poison-bad world for the romancer,' for sticking with iron courage to the graveside, and refusing to engage in work less resolute, and more easy.

Yes, more easy; for it *is* more easy – if more degrading – to write a certain kind of novel. To take a fanciful instance, it is more easy to write the history of Miss Perfect: how, upon the death of her parents, she comes to reside in the village, and lives there mildly and sedately; and how one day, in the course of her walk abroad, she is noticed by the squire's lady, who straightway transports her to the Hall. And, of course, she soon becomes mighty well with the family, and the squire's son becomes enamoured of her. Then the clouds must gather: and a villain lord comes on the scene to bombard her virtue with clumsy artillery. Finding after months that her virtue dwells in an impregnable citadel, he turns to, and jibes and goads the young squire to the fighting point. And, presto! there they are, hard at it with bare steel, on the Norman beach, of a drizzling morning; and the squire is just pressing hot upon my lord, when – it's hey! for the old love, and ho! for the new – out rushes my Miss Perfect to our great amazement, and falls between the swords down on the stinging sands, in the sight of the toiling sea. Now I maintain, that a novel woven of these meagre threads, and set out in three volumes and a brave binding, would put up a good front at Mudie's; would become, it too, after a while, morality packed in a box. For nowadays we seem to nourish our morals with the thinnest milk and water, with a good dose of sugar added, and not a suspicion of lemon at all.

You will note that the letter-writer says, the '*Anglo-Saxon* world' – Great Britain, say! and the United States; and it is well to keep in mind this distinction. In France, for example, people appear eager to watch how art triumphs over any matter. 'Charles Baudelaire,' says Hamerton, 'had the poetical organization with all its worst inconveniences;' but one inconvenience he had not – the inconvenience of a timid public not interested in form, and with a profound hatred of the unusual: a public from which Edgar Poe, Beddoes, and Francis Saltus (to name but three) suffered – how poignantly! Let us cling by all means to our George Meredith, our Henry James – our Miss Rhoda Broughton, if you will; but then let us try, if we cannot be towards others, unlike these, if not encouraging, at the least not actively hostile and harassing, when they go out in the black night to follow their own sullen will-o'-the-wisps.

'The Barber' (1893)

JOHN GRAY

Thanatos and Eros meet in this startling exploration of
murderous impulses.

I dreamed I was a barber; and there went
Beneath my hand, oh! names extravagant.
Beneath my trembling fingers, many a mask
Of many a pleasant girl. It was my task
To gild their hair, carefully, strand by strand;
To paint their eyebrows with a timid hand;
To draw a bodkin, from a vase of kohl,
Through the closed lashes; pencils from a bowl
Of Sepia to paint them underneath;
To blow upon their eyes with a soft breath.
Then lay them back and watched the leaping bands.

The dream grew vague. I moulded with my hands
The mobile breasts, the valley; and the waist
I touched; and pigments reverently placed
Upon their thighs in sapient spots and stains,
Beryls and crysolites and diaphanes,
And gems whose hot harsh names are never said,
I was a masseur; and my fingers bled
With wonder as I touched their awful limbs.

Suddenly, in the marble trough, there seems
O, last of my pale mistresses, Sweetness!
A twy-lipped scarlet pansy. My caress
Tinges thy steel-gray eyes to violet.
Adown thy body skips the pit-a-pat
Of treatment once heard in a hospital
For plagues that fascinate, but half appal.

So, at the sound, the blood of one stood cold.
My chaste hair ripened into sudden gold.
The throat, the shoulders, swelled and were uncouth
The breasts rose up and offered each a mouth.
And on the belly pallid blushes crept,
That maddened me, until I laughed and wept.

'The Ballad of a Barber' (1896)

AUBREY BEARDSLEY

*Another demon barber – Beardsley's poem is a tragi-comic tale of
artifice, sexual perversion and morbidity. A decadent classic.*

Here is the tale of Carrousel,
The barber of Meridian Street.
He cut, and coiffed, and shaved so well,
That all the world was at his feet.

The King, the Queen, and all the Court,
To no one else would trust their hair,
And reigning belles of every sort
Owed their successes to his care.

With carriage and with cabriolet
Daily Meridian Street was blocked,
Like bees about a bright bouquet
The beaux about his doorway flocked.

Such was his art he could with ease
Curl wit into the dullest face;
Or to a goddess of old Greece
Add a new wonder and a grace.

All powders, paints, and subtle dyes,
And costliest scents that men distil,
And rare pomades, forgot their price
And marvelled at his splendid skill.

AUBREY BEARDSLEY.

The curling irons in his hand
Almost grew quick enough to speak,
The razor was a magic wand
That understood the softest cheek.

Yet with no pride his heart was moved;
He was so modest in his ways!
His daily task was all he loved,
And now and then a little praise.

An equal care he would bestow
On problems simple or complex;
And nobody had seen him show
A preference for either sex.

How came it then one summer day,
Coiffing the daughter of the King,
He lengthened out the least delay
And loitered in his hairdressing?

The Princess was a pretty child,
Thirteen years old, or thereabout.
She was as joyous and as wild
As spring flowers when the sun is out.

Her gold hair fell down to her feet
And hung about her pretty eyes;
She was as lyrical and sweet
As one of Schubert's melodies.

Three times the barber curled a lock,
And thrice he straightened it again;
And twice the irons scorched her frock,
And twice he stumbled in her train.

His fingers lost their cunning quite,
His ivory combs obeyed no more;
Something or other dimmed his sight,
And moved mysteriously the floor.

He leant upon the toilet table,
His fingers fumbled in his breast;
He felt as foolish as a fable,
And feeble as a pointless jest.

He snatched a bottle of Cologne,
And broke the neck between his hands;
He felt as if he was alone,
And mighty as a king's commands.

The Princess gave a little scream,
Carrousel's cut was sharp and deep;
He left her softly as a dream
That leaves a sleeper to his sleep.

He left the room on pointed feet;
Smiling that things had gone so well.
They hanged him in Meridian Street.
You pray in vain for Carrousel.

'The Visit' (1899)

ERNEST DOWSON

Death is characterised as tender, benevolent and welcoming, which makes this very short story all the more unsettling.

As though I were still struggling through the meshes of some riotous dream, I heard his knock upon the door. As in a dream, I bade him enter, but with his entry, I awoke. Yet when he entered it seemed to me that I was dreaming, for there was nothing strange in that supreme and sorrowful smile which shone through the mask which I knew. And just as though I had not always been afraid of him I said:

'Welcome.'

And he said very simply, 'I am here.'

Dreaming I had thought myself, but the reproachful sorrow of his smile showed me that I was awake. Then dared I open my eyes and I saw my old body on the bed, and the room in which I had grown so tired, and in the middle of the room the pan of charcoal which still smouldered. And dimly I remembered my great weariness and the lost whiteness of Lalage and last year's snows; and these things had been agonies.

Darkly, as in a dream, I wondered why they gave me no more hurt, as I looked at my old body on the bed; why, they were like old maids' fancies (as I looked at my grey body on the bed of my agonies) – like silly toys of children that fond mothers lay up in lavender (as I looked at the twisted limbs of my old body), for these things had been agonies.

But all my wonder was gone when I looked again into the eyes of my guest, and I said:

'I have wanted you all my life.'

Then said Death (and what reproachful tenderness was shadowed in his obscure smile):

'You had only to call.'

'Viol d'Amor' (1894)

COUNT ERIC STANISLAUS STENBOCK

A very strange story from a very strange man. Stenbock is little-known, and his few published works are now incredibly rare. It is a delight to include him in this anthology.

One time there was much in vogue a peculiarly sweet-toned kind of violin, or rather, to be accurate, something between a viola and a violoncello. Now they are no longer made. This is the history of the last one that was ever made, I think. This somewhat singular story might in some way explain why they are made no longer. But though I am a poetess, and consequently inclined to believe in the unlikely, this I do not suppose was the history of Viol d'Amors in general. I may add, by way of prefix, that its peculiar sweetness of tone was produced by the duplicated reverberation of strings below, with yet another reverberation within the sounding-board. But to my story.

I was once in Freiburg – Freiburg in Baden, I mean. I went one Sunday to High Mass at the Cathedral. Beethoven's glorious Mass in C was magnificently rendered by a string quartette. I was specially impressed by the first violin, a dignified, middle-aged man, with a singularly handsome face, reminding one of the portraits of Leonardo da Vinci. He was dressed in a medieval-looking black robe; and he played with an inspiration such as I have seldom, if ever, heard. There was likewise a most beautiful boy's treble. Boys' voices, lovely in their 'timbre' as nothing else, are generally somewhat wanting in their expression. This one united the most exquisite 'timbre' with the most complete possible expression. I was going to stay in Freiburg some time, as I knew people there. The first violinist had aroused my curiosity. I learnt that he was an Italian, a Florentine, of the ancient noble family of da Ripoli. But he was now a maker of musical instruments, not very well off – who nevertheless played at the Cathedral for love, not money; also that the beautiful treble was his youngest son, and he was a

STVDIES OF DEATH

STORIES BY

S. E. STENBOCK.

widower with five children. As he interested me, I sought to procure an introduction, which I succeeded in getting without difficulty.

He lived in one of those beautiful old houses which linger still in towns like Freiburg; he seemed somewhat surprised that an Englishwoman should go out of her way to visit him. Fortunately I was familiar with Italian, being myself an Italian on the mother's side, and was at that time on my way to Italy. He received me with much affability. I was ushered into a long Gothic room, done in black oak: there was a very beautiful Gothic window, which was open. It was spring-time, and the most delightful weather. There was a strong scent of May about the room, emanating from a hawthorn-tree immediately opposite the window, which had the extraordinary peculiarity of bearing red and white blossoms at the same time. The room was full of all sorts of odds and ends of things – caskets, vessels, embroideries-all exquisitely artistic. He told me these were executed by a son and daughter of his. We began to interest one another, and had a long talk. As we were talking, in walked a tall, grave-looking young man. He was of the pure Etruscan type – dark, and indeed somewhat sombre.

With a perturbed air, not noticing me, he suddenly made this singular remark, 'Saturn is in conjunction with the moon: I fear that ill may betide Guido.'

'This is my son Andrea,' his father explained, 'my eldest son; he goes in much for astronomy, and indeed also for astrology, in which you probably do not believe.'

At that moment in walked another young man. This was the second son, Giovanni. He was also dark, like his brother, and tall, but had a very pleasing smile. He reminded me rather of the portrait of Andrea del Sarto. It was he who manufactured – to use the word in its proper sense – these beautiful objects which were lying about the table. After him came in two sisters: the elder, whose name was Anastasia, was a tall, stately girl, with dark hair and grey eyes, but pale face: very much like the type we are familiar with from the pictures of Dante Gabriel Rossetti. The younger sister was quite different: she was fair, but fair in the Italian manner: that glorious, ivory-white complexion so different from the pink and white of the North. Her hair was of that glorious red-gold colour which we see in Titian's pictures, but her eyes were dark. Her name was Liperata. It appears Anastasia was the eldest of the family, then came Andrea and Giovanni, then Liperata, and lastly, Guido, whom I had not seen as yet.

I omitted to mention, though it does not seem here of any significance at all, that Anastasia wore a blue gown of somewhat stiff medieval cut, but very graceful all the same. I learnt afterwards it was both designed and made by herself.

Presently there entered the room a boy of about fourteen. This was Guido. He was fairer than his brothers, though also somewhat of the Etruscan type, and was not so tall for his age. He looked singularly fragile and delicate. His complexion was more delicate than a rose-petal: he had those long, supple, sensitive hands which indicate the born musician. His somewhat long hair, of a shade of brown, had a shadow of gold on it, as if it had been golden once. But in his strange-coloured eyes, which were grey-blue, streaked with yellow bars, there was a far-off look, like a light not of this world, shining on a slowly-rippling river of music. He went straight to the window, also not noticing there was a stranger in the room, and said, 'Ah, how beautiful the May-tree is! I shall only see it bloom once more.' He seemed indeed to be looking through the blooming hawthorn at that pale planet Saturn, which then was, for it, singularly large and brilliant. Andrea shuddered, but Giovanni bent down and kissed him, and said, 'What, Guido, another fit of melancholia?'

As you may imagine, I was interested in this singular family, and soon our acquaintance ripened into intimacy. It was to Anastasia that I was specially drawn, and she to me. Anastasia inherited the musical tastes of her father, and was herself no mean executant on the violin.

Andrea was not only occupied with astronomy and astrology, but even with alchemy and such like things, and occult sciences generally.

The whole family was very superstitious. They seemed to take astrology and magic as matters of course. But Andrea was by far the most superstitious of them all. It was Giovanni who was the breadwinner of the family, together with his special sister, Liperata, who assisted him in his work, and herself did the most charming embroideries. The only thing was that their materials were too costly, and required a large outlay to be made before they could sell anything.

For though the musical instruments the father produced were super-excellent of their kind, and fetched large prices, he took so much care about his work that he was sometimes years in producing one violin. He was then absorbed in one idea, in producing a Viol d'Amor, an instrument which he said was the most beautiful in all the world, and which had unjustly fallen into disuse. And his Viol d'Amor was to excel all others that had ever been made. He had left Florence, he said, because he could not stand this great Republic (for though of one of the most ancient noble families, he was an ardent Republican) being converted into the capital of a tenth-rate monarchy. 'They will be taking Rome next,' he said. And he did not know that what he was saying was soon to come true.

They were not well off, certainly, but it was Anastasia who managed the household and cared for every one. And she was the most excellent of manageresses. And so their life was very simple, but nevertheless was elegant and refined.

I very often enjoyed their simple, truly Italian hospitality, recompensing them by purchasing some specimens of Giovanni's excellent workmanship, and a violin from the old Signor da Ripoli, which I have still, and would not part with for the world. Though, alas! I myself cannot play upon it. To cut a long story short, I had to go on with my journey, but I did not wholly lose sight of them, so to speak, and I corresponded frequently with Anastasia.

One day, just about a year afterwards, I received the following letter from Anastasia:-

'Dear Cecilia, – A great calamity has fallen upon us. It is so out of the common that you would hardly believe it. Of course you know how my father is devoted to his Viol d'Amor. You also know that we are all rather superstitious, but none to the same degree as Andrea. It appears that one day Andrea was poring into some old book, which was in that mongrel tongue, half Latin and half Italian, before the days of Dante, when he came across a passage (you know, I know nothing about the manufacture of musical instruments; but it appears that leather thongs are necessary to procure the complete vibration of the Viol d'Amor). In this passage it said that preternatural sweetness of tone could be procured if the thongs were made of the skin of those who loved the maker most. – [I had heard of this superstition before: I think there is some story in connection with Paganini of a similar nature, but nevertheless quite different. For as the legend goes about Paganini, the strings of a violin were made of the entrails of a person, which necessitated their murder; but here it would appear from the rest of the letter it did not do so, and was a freewill offering.] – Andrea conceived the fantastic idea of cutting off part of his own skin and having it tanned unbeknown to our father, telling him he had got it from the Clinic, because he had heard human leather was the best. To effect this he had to invoke the assistance of Giovanni, who, as you know, is so skilful with all instruments, and is also, as perhaps you do not know, a most skilful surgeon.

'Giovanni, not to be outdone by his brother, performed the same operation on himself. They were obliged to confide in me, and, as you know, I am very good as a nurse, and clever at bandages and such like. So I managed, with a little bandaging, and nursing, and sewing up the scars, to get them quite well again in a very short time. Of course no word of this was ever said to Liperata or Guido. And now comes the dreadful part of my story. How Guido could have divined anything I cannot understand. The only explanation I can offer is this. He is a very studious boy, and very fond of poring into the old books in Andrea's library. He might have seen the same passage, and with his extraordinary quick intuition have guessed. Anyhow he appears to have gone to some quack Jew doctor, and had a portion of his skin cut off in the same manner, and brought the skin to his brothers to be dealt with in the same way, which it was. The operation had been performed badly, and, as you know, the child is very delicate, and it has had the most disastrous results. He is hopelessly ill, and we do not know what to do. Of course we cannot tell our father. It is equally impossible to tell a doctor. Fortunately our father does not believe in doctors and trusts in us. It is a good thing all three of us know something of medical science: I think things are getting a little better. He rallied a little yesterday, and asked to be taken from his bed to the sofa in the long room. At his own request he was placed just opposite the May-tree, with the window open. This seemed to revive him. He became, comparatively speaking, quite animated, especially when a slight wind blew some of the red and white blossoms on to his coverlet. Giovanni and I have some hope, but Andrea has not. Liperata of course does not understand what it all means. Nor does our father, who is intensely anxious about Guido, whom he loves best of. us all. – Ever affectionately,

'Anastasia'

'P.S. – Good news at last! the Viol d'Amor is completed. Father came down and played it to us. Oh! what a divine tone it has! Guido first burst into tears, and then seemed to grow quite well again for some time afterwards. Father left the Viol d'Amor with me, that I should play to Guido whenever he wished it. Yes, there is hope after all, whatever Andrea may say.'

Not long afterwards I received another letter from Anastasia in deep mourning. It ran thus:-

'The worst has happened. Last Friday, after having been for several days considerably better, Guido seemed almost himself again. I was alone with him in the long room. (One thinks of trivialities in great grief; I was wearing that same blue dress I had on when I first saw you.) There was a wind, also rain, which pattered against the window-pane, and the wind blew the blossoms of the May-tree like red-white snow to the ground. This seemed to depress Guido. He begged me to sing to him, and accompany myself on the Viol d'Amor. "It is so sweet of tone," he said, with a sweet, sad smile. "I am rather tired, though I do not feel much pain now. I shall not see the hawthorn bloom again."

'I began to sing an old Etruscan ballad-one of those songs that linger about the country parts of Tuscany, of a very simple, plaintive cadence, accompanied softly on the Viol d'Amor. It would be soothing, I thought, at any rate. And it was. Guido laid his head back and closed his eyes. Gradually the rain ceased and the wind stilled. Guido looked up. "That is better," he said, "I was afraid of the wind and the rain; and you stopped them with the Viol d'Amor! Look! the moon is beginning to shine again." It was a full moon, and it shone through the hawthorn-tree, making strange shadows on the window, and one ray shot direct on Guido's pale face. "Go on singing," he said faintly. So I sang on, and played on the Viol d'Amor. I felt some dreadful presentiment. I dared not stop singing and playing. It seemed that a shadow literally crept through the doorway, and came up to the bed, and bent over it. Then suddenly all the strings of the Viol d'Amor snapped! A strange wail seemed to come out of the sounding-board. I dropped it, and looked! Then I saw it was too late.

******

'Father took the Viol d'Amor and broke it in pieces, and cast it into the fire. His silent agony is too terrible to describe. I cannot tell you any more now.'

I was in Freiburg once again, and of course the first thing I did was to go and see my old friends. The Signor da Ripoli was very much aged. He still plays in the Cathedral. Did he, or did he not, ever know what had happened? Anyhow, he has made no further attempt to construct a Viol d'Amor; nor may the word even be mentioned in his presence.

Giovanni and Liperata have gone back to Italy, where they have set up a workshop for themselves. It is rumoured that Liperata is shortly to be married. But Anastasia remains with her father. I do not think that she will ever marry. Andrea has become a victim to settled melancholy. He lives quite by himself in a lonely tower. It was he who had the following inscription put on Guido's tomb:

'La musica e l' Amor che mouve
il Sole e l'altre Stelle.'

'The Falling of the Leaves' (1889)

W. B. YEATS

W. B. Yeats escaped the 1890s relatively unscathed, unlike most of his circle, who nearly all succumbed to death, insanity or Catholicism within a decade. 'The Falling of the Leaves' *reflects on the changing of the seasons, not the ending of an era.*

Autumn is over the long leaves that love us,
And over the mice in the barley sheaves;
Yellow the leaves of the rowan above us,
And yellow the wet wild-strawberry leaves.

The hour of the waning of love has beset us,
And weary and worn are our sad souls now;
Let us part, ere the season of passion forget us,
With a kiss and a tear on thy drooping brow.

'The Dying of Francis Donne: A Study' (1896)

ERNEST DOWSON

Dowson wrote only a few short stories and this is his finest. His love-song to death is a shockingly direct work.

'*Memento homo, quia pulvis es et in pulverem reverteris*'

I

He had lived so long in the meditation of death, visited it so often in others, studied it with such persistency, with a sentiment in which horror and fascination mingled; but it had always been, as it were, an objective, alien fact, remote from himself and his own life. So that it was in a sudden flash, quite too stupefying to admit in the first instance of terror, that knowledge of his mortality dawned on him. There was absurdity in the idea too.

'I, Francis Donne, thirty-five and some months old, am going to die,' he said to himself; and fantastically he looked at his image in the glass, and sought, but quite vainly, to find some change in it which should account for this incongruity, just as, searching in his analytical habit into the recesses of his own mind, he could find no such alteration of his inner consciousness as would explain or justify his plain conviction. And quickly, with reason and casuistry, he sought to rebut that conviction.

The quickness of his mind – it had never seemed to him so nimble, so exquisite a mechanism of syllogism and deduction – was contraposed against his blind instinct of the would-be self-deceiver, in a conflict to which the latter brought something of desperation, the fierce, agonized desperation of a hunted animal at bay. But piece by piece the chain of evidence was strengthened. That subtile and agile mind of his, with its special knowledge, cut clean through the shrinking protests of instinct, removing them as surely and as remorselessly, he reflected in the image most natural to him, as the keen blades of his surgical knives had removed malignant ulcers.

'I, Francis Donne, am going to die,' he repeated, and, presently, '*I am going to die soon;* in a few months, in six perhaps, certainly in a year.'

Once more, curiously, but this time with a sense of neutrality, as he had often diagnosed a patient, he turned to the mirror. Was it his fancy, or, perhaps, only for the vague light that he seemed to discover a strange grey tone about his face?

But he had always been a man of a very sallow complexion.

There were a great many little lines, like pen-scratches, scarring the parchment-like skin beneath the keen eyes: doubtless, of late, these had multiplied, become more noticeable, even when his face was in repose.

But, of late, what with his growing practice, his lectures, his writing; all the unceasing labour, which his ambitions entailed, might well have aged him somewhat. That dull, immutable pain, which had first directed his attention from his studies, his investigations, his profession, to his corporal self, the actual Francis Donne, that pain which he would so gladly have called inexplicable, but could explain so precisely, had ceased for the moment. Nerves, fancies! How long it was since he had taken any rest! He had often intended to give himself a holiday, but something had always intervened. But he would do so now, yes, almost immediately; a long, long holiday – he would grudge nothing – somewhere quite out of the way, somewhere, where there was fishing; in Wales, or perhaps in Brittany; that would surely set him right.

And even while he promised himself this necessary relaxation in the immediate future, as he started on his afternoon round, in the background of his mind there lurked the date, was, as it were, some tardy sacrifice, almost hypocritical, which he offered to powers who might not be propitiated.

Once in his neat brougham, the dull pain began again; but by an effort of will he put it away from him. In the brief interval from house to house – he had some dozen visits to make – he occupied himself with a medical paper, glanced at the notes of a lecture he was giving that evening at a certain Institute on the 'Limitations of Medicine.'

He was late, very late for dinner, and his man, Bromgrove, greeted him with a certain reproachfulness, in which he traced, or seemed to trace, a half-patronizing sense of pity. He reminded himself that on more than one occasion, of late, Bromgrove's manner had perplexed him. He was glad to rebuke the man irritably on some pretext, to dismiss him from the room, and he hurried, without appetite, through the cold or overdone food which was the reward of his tardiness.

His lecture over, he drove out to South Kensington, to attend a reception at the house of a great man – great not only in the scientific world, but also in the world of letters. There was some of the excitement of success in his eyes as he made his way, with smiles and bows, in acknowledgment of many compliments, through the crowded rooms. For Francis Donne's lectures – those of them which were not entirely for the initiated – had grown into the importance of a social function. They had almost succeeded in making science fashionable, clothing its dry bones in a garment of so elegantly literary a pattern. But even in the ranks of the profession it was only the envious, the unsuccessful, who ventured to say that Donne had sacrificed doctrine to popularity, that his science was, in their contemptuous parlance, 'mere literature.'

Yes, he had been very successful, as the world counts success, and his consciousness of this fact, and the influence of the lights, the crowd, the voices, was like absinthe on his tired spirit. He had forgotten, or thought he had forgotten, the phantom of the last few days, the phantom which was surely waiting for him at home.

But he was reminded by a certain piece of news which late in the evening fluttered the now diminished assembly: the quite sudden death of an eminent surgeon, expected there that night, an acquaintance of his own, and more or less of each one of the little, intimate group which tarried to discuss it. With sympathy, with a certain awe, they spoke of him, Donne and others; and both the awe and the sympathy were genuine.

But as he drove home, leaning back in his carriage, in a discouragement, in a lethargy, which was only partly due to physical reaction, he saw visibly underneath their regret – theirs and his own – the triumphant assertion of life, the egoism of instinct. They were sorry, but oh, they were glad! royally

glad, that it was another, and not they themselves whom something mysterious had of a sudden snatched away from his busy career, his interests, perhaps from all intelligence; at least, from all the pleasant sensuousness of life, the joy of the visible world, into darkness. And honestly dared not to blame it. How many times had not he, Francis Donne himself experienced it, that egoistic assertion of life in the presence of the dead – the poor, irremediable dead? – And now, he was only good to give it to others.

Latterly, he had been in the habit of subduing sleeplessness with injections of morphia, indeed in infinitesimal quantities. But to-night, although he was more than usually restless and awake, by a strong effort of reasonableness he resisted his impulse to take out the little syringe. The pain was at him again with the same dull and stupid insistence; in its monotony, losing some of the nature of pain and becoming a mere nervous irritation. But he was aware that it would not continue like that. Daily, almost hourly, it would gather strength and cruelty; the moments of respite from it would become rarer, would cease. From a dull pain it would become an acute pain, and then a torture, and then an agony, and then a madness. And in those last days, what peace might be his would be the peace of morphia, so that it was essential that, for the moment, he should not abuse the drug.

And as he knew that sleep was far away from him, he propped himself up with two pillows, and by the light of a strong reading lamp settled himself to read. He had selected the work of a distinguished German *savant* upon the cardiac functions, and a short treatise of his own, which was covered with recent annotations, in his crabbed handwriting, upon 'Aneurism of the Heart.' He read avidly, and against his own deductions, once more his instinct raised a vain protest. At last he threw the volumes aside, and lay with his eyes shut, without, however, extinguishing the light. A terrible sense of helplessness overwhelmed him; he was seized with an immense and heartbreaking pity for poor humanity as personified in himself; and, for the first time since he had ceased to be a child, he shed puerile tears.

II

The faces of his acquaintance, the faces of the students at his lectures, the faces of Francis Donne's colleagues at the hospital, were altered; were, at least, sensibly altered to his morbid self-consciousness. In every one whom he encountered, he detected, or fancied that he detected, an attitude of evasion, a hypocritical air of ignoring a fact that was obvious and unpleasant. Was it so obvious, then, the hidden horror which he carried incessantly about him? Was his secret, which he would still guard so jealously, become a by-word and an anecdote in his little world? And a great rage consumed him against the inexorable and inscrutable forces which had made him to destroy him; against himself, because of his proper impotence; and, above all, against the living, the millions who would remain when he was no longer, the living, of whom many would regret him (some of them his personality, and more, his skill), because he could see under all the unconscious hypocrisy of their sorrow, the exultant self-satisfaction of their survival.

And with his burning sense of helplessness, of a certain bitter injustice in things, a sense of shame mingled; all the merely physical dishonour of death shaping itself to his sick and morbid fancy into a violent symbol of what was, as it were, an actual *moral* or intellectual dishonour. Was not death, too, inevitable and natural an operation as it was, essentially a process to undergo apart and hide jealously, as much as other natural and ignoble processes of the body?

And the animal, who steals away to an uttermost place in the forest, who gives up his breath in a solitude and hides his dying like a shameful thing, – might he not offer an example that it would be well for the dignity of poor humanity to follow?

Since Death is coming to me, said Francis Donne to himself, let me meet it, a stranger in a strange land, with only strange faces round me and the kind indifference of strangers, instead of the intolerable pity of friends.

III

On the bleak and wave-tormented coast of Finistère, somewhere between Quiberon and Fouesnant, he reminded himself of a little fishing-village: a few scattered houses (one of them being an *auberge* at which ten years ago he had spent a night), collected round a poor little grey church. Thither Francis Donne went, without leave-takings or explanation, almost secretly, giving but the vaguest indications of the length or direction of his absence. And there for many days he dwelt, in the cottage which he had hired, with one old Breton woman for his sole attendant, in a state of mind which, after all the years of energy, of ambitious labour, was almost peace.

Bleak and grey it had been, when he had visited it of old, in the late autumn; but now the character, the whole colour of the country was changed. It was brilliant with the promise of summer, and the blue Atlantic, which in winter churned with its long crested waves so boisterously below the little white lighthouse, which warned mariners (alas! so vainly), against the shark-like cruelty of the rocks, now danced and glittered in the sunshine, rippled with feline caresses round the hulls of the fishing-boats whose brown sails floated so idly in the faint air.

Above the village, on a grassy slope, whose green was almost lurid, Francis Donne lay, for many silent hours, looking out at the placid sea, which could yet be so ferocious, at the low violet line of the Island of Groix, which alone interrupted the monotony of sky and ocean.

He had brought many books with him but he read in them rarely; and when physical pain gave him a respite for thought, he thought almost of nothing. His thought was for a long time a lethargy and a blank.

Now and again he spoke with some of the inhabitants. They were a poor and hardy, but a kindly race: fishers and the wives of fishers, whose children would grow up and become fishermen and the wives of fishermen in their turn. Most of them had wrestled with death; it was always so near to them that hardly one of them feared it; they were fatalists, with the grim and resigned fatalism of the poor, of the poor who live with the treachery of the sea.

Francis Donne visited the little cemetery, and counted the innumerable crosses which testified to the havoc which the sea had wrought. Some of the graves were nameless; holding the bodies of strange seamen which the waves had tossed ashore.

'And in a little time I shall lie here,' he said to himself; 'and here as

well as elsewhere,' he added with a shrug, assuming, and, for once, almost
sincerely, the stoicism of his surroundings, 'and as lief to-day as to-morrow.'

On the whole, the days were placid; there were even moments when,
as though he had actually drunk in renewed vigour from that salt sea air,
the creative force of the sun, he was tempted to doubt his grievous
knowledge, to make fresh plans for life. But these were fleeting moments,
and the reaction from them was terrible. Each day his hold on life was
visibly more slender, and the people of the village saw, and with a rough
sympathy, which did not offend him, allowed him to perceive that they
saw, the rapid growth and the inevitableness of his end.

IV

But if the days were not without their pleasantness, the nights were always
horrible – a torture of the body and an agony of the spirit. Sleep was far
away, and the brain, which had been lulled till the evening, would awake,
would grow electric with life and take strange and abominable flights into
the darkness of the pit, into the black night of the unknowable and the
unknown.

And interminably, during those nights which seemed eternity, Francis
Donne questioned and examined into the nature of that Thing, which
stood, a hooded figure beside his bed, with a menacing hand raised to
beckon him so peremptorily from all that lay within his consciousness.

He had been all his life absorbed in science; he had dissected, how
many bodies? and in what anatomy had he ever found a soul? Yet if his
avocations, his absorbing interest in physical phenomena had made him
somewhat a materialist, it had been almost without his consciousness. The
sensible, visible world of matter had loomed so large to him, that merely
to know that had seemed to him sufficient. All that might conceivably lie
outside it, he had, without negation, been content to regard as outside his
province.

And now, in his weakness, in the imminence of approaching
dissolution, his purely physical knowledge seemed but a vain possession,
and he turned with a passionate interest to what had been said and believed
from time immemorial by those who had concentrated their intelligence

on that strange essence, which might after all be the essence of one's personality, which might be that sublimated consciousness – the Soul – actually surviving the infamy of the grave?

> Animula, vagula, blandula!
> Hospes comesque corporis,
> Quae nunc abibis in loca?
> Pallidula, rigida, nudula.

Ah, the question! It was a harmony, perhaps (as, who had maintained? whom the Platonic Socrates in the 'Phaedo' had not too successfully refuted), a harmony of life, which was dissolved when life was over? Or, perhaps, as how many metaphysicians had held both before and after a sudden great hope, perhaps too generous to be true, had changed and illuminated, to countless millions, the inexorable figure of Death a principle, indeed, immortal, which came and went, passing through many corporal conditions until it was ultimately resolved into the great mind, pervading all things? Perhaps? But what scanty consolation, in all such theories, to the poor body, racked with pain and craving peace, to the tortured spirit of self-consciousness so achingly anxious not to be lost.

And he turned from these speculations to what was, after all, a possibility like the others; the faith of the simple, of these fishers with whom he lived, which was also the faith of his own childhood, which, indeed, he had never repudiated, whose practices he had simply discarded, as one discards puerile garments when one comes to man's estate. And he remembered, with the vividness with which, in moments of great anguish, one remembers things long ago familiar, forgotten though they may have been for years, the triumphant declarations of the Church:

'*Omnes quidem resurgemus, sed non omnes immutabimur. In momento, in ictu oculi, in novissima tuba: canet enim tuba: et mortui resurgent incorrupti, et nos immutabimur. Oportet enim corruptibile hoc induere immortalitatem. Cum autem mortale hoc induerit immortalitatem tunc fiet sermo qui scriptus est: Absorpta est mors in victoria. Ubi est, mors, victoria tua? Ubi est, mors, stimulus tuus?*'

Ah, for the certitude of that! of that victorious confutation of the apparent destruction of sense and spirit in a common ruin. But it was a possibility like the rest; and had it not more need than the rest to be more than a possibility, if it would be a consolation, in that it promised more? And he gave it up, turning his face to the wall, lay very still, imagining himself already stark and cold, his eyes closed, his jaw closely tied (lest the ignoble changes which had come to him should be too ignoble), while he waited until the narrow boards, within which he should lie, had been nailed together, and the bearers were ready to convey him into the corruption which was to be his part.

And as the window-pane grew light with morning, he sank into a drugged, unrestful sleep, from which he would awake some hours later with eyes more sunken and more haggard cheeks. And that was the pattern of many nights.

V

One day he seemed to wake from a night longer and more troubled than usual, a night which had, perhaps, been many nights and days, perhaps even weeks; a night of an ever-increasing agony, in which he was only dimly conscious at rare intervals of what was happening, or of the figures coming and going around his bed: the doctor from a neighbouring town, who had stayed by him unceasingly, easing his paroxysms with the little merciful syringe; the soft, practised hands of a sister of charity about his pillow; even the face of Bromgrove, for whom doubtless he had sent, when he had foreseen the utter helplessness which was at hand.

He opened his eyes, and seemed to discern a few blurred figures against the darkness of the closed shutters through which one broad ray filtered in; but he could not distinguish their faces, and he closed his eyes once more. An immense and ineffable tiredness had come over him that this – *this* was Death; this was the thing against which he had cried and revolted; the horror from which he would have escaped; this utter luxury of physical exhaustion, this calm, this release.

The corporal capacity of smiling had passed from him, but he would fain have smiled.

And for a few minutes of singular mental lucidity, all his life flashed before him in a new relief; his childhood, his adolescence, the people whom he had known; his mother, who had died when he was a boy, of a malady from which, perhaps, a few years later, his skill would had saved her; the friend of his youth who had shot himself for so little reason; the girl whom he had loved, but who had not loved him. All that was distorted in life was adjusted and justified in the light of his sudden knowledge. *Beati mortui* and then the great tiredness swept over him once more, and a fainter consciousness, in which he could yet just dimly hear, as in a dream, the sound of Latin prayers, and feel the application of the oils upon all the issues and approaches of his wearied sense; then utter unconsciousness, while pulse and heart gradually grew fainter until both ceased. And that was all.

'A Literary Causerie:
On a Book of Verses' (1896)

ARTHUR SYMONS

Arthur Symons would end each issue of the Savoy *with a 'Literary Causerie'*
on writers he admired. The unnamed focus of issue four's causerie was Ernest
Dowson, who although still alive at the time, is treated to a sort of premature
eulogy. It is a wistful, sad and lovely portrait.

A book of delicate, mournful, almost colourless, but very fragrant verses
was lately published by a young poet whom I have the privilege to know
somewhat intimately. Whether a book so essentially poetic, and at the
same time so fragile in its hold on outward things, is likely to appeal very
much to the general public, for which verse is still supposed to be written,
it scarcely interests me to conjecture. It is a matter of more legitimate
speculation, what sort of person would be called up before the mind's eye
of any casual reader, as the author of love-poetry so reverent and so
disembodied. A very ghostly lover, I suppose, wandering in a land of
perpetual twilight, holding a whispered 'colloque sentimental' with the
ghost of an old love:

'Dans le vieux parc solitaire et glacé

Deux spectres ont évoqué le passé.'

That is not how I have seen my friend, for the most part; and the
contrast between the man as I have seen him and the writer of verses as I
read them, is to me the most attractive interest of a book which I find
singularly attractive. He will not mind, I know, if I speak of him with
some of that frankness which we reserve usually for the dead, or with
which we sometimes honour our enemies; for he is of a complete
indifference to these things, as I shall assure myself over again before
these lines are printed.

I do not remember the occasion of our first meeting, but I remember

seeing him casually, at railway-stations, in a semi-literary tavern which once had a fantastic kind of existence, and sometimes, at night, in various parts of the Temple, before I was more than slightly his acquaintance. I was struck then by a look and manner of pathetic charm, a sort of Keats-like face, the face of a demoralized Keats, and by something curious in the contrast of a manner exquisitely refined, with an appearance generally somewhat dilapidated. That impression was only accentuated, later on, when I came to know him, and the manner of his life, much more intimately. I think I may date my first real impression of what one calls 'the real man' – as if it were more real than the poet of the disembodied verses! – from an evening in which he first introduced me to those charming supper-houses, open all night through, the cabmen's shelters. There were four of us, two in evening dress, and we were welcomed, cordially and without comment, at a little place near the Langham; and, I recollect, very hospitably entertained. He was known there, and I used to think he was always at his best in a cabmen's shelter. Without a certain sordidness in his surroundings, he was never quite comfortable, never quite himself; and at those places you are obliged to drink nothing stronger than coffee or tea. I liked to see him occasionally, for a change, drinking nothing stronger than coffee or tea. At Oxford, I believe, his favourite form of intoxication had been haschisch; afterwards he gave up this somewhat elaborate experiment in visionary sensations for readier means of oblivion; but he returned to it, I remember, for at least one afternoon, in a company of which I had been the gatherer, and of which I was the host. The experience was not a very successful one; it ended in what should have been its first symptom, immoderate laughter. It was disappointing, and my charming, expectant friends, disappointed.

Always, perhaps a little consciously, but at least always sincerely, in search of new sensations, my friend found what was for him the supreme sensation in a very passionate and tender adoration of the most escaping of all ideals, the ideal of youth. Cherished, as I imagine, first only in the abstract, this search after the immature, the ripening graces which time can but spoil in the ripening, found itself at the journey's end, as some of his friends thought, a little prematurely. I was never of their opinion. I only saw twice, and for a few moments only, the young girl to whom most of his verses were to be written, and whose presence in his life may be held to account for much of that astonishing contrast between the broad outlines of his life and work. The situation seemed to me of the most exquisite and appropriate impossibility. She had the gift of evoking, and, in its way, of retaining, all that was most delicate, sensitive, shy, typically poetic, in a nature which I can only compare to a weedy garden, its grass trodden down by many feet, but with one small, carefully-tended flower-bed, luminous with lilies. I used to think, sometimes, of Verlaine and his 'girl-wife,' the one really profound passion, certainly, of that passionate career; the charming, child-like creature, to whom he looked back, at the end of his life, with an unchanged tenderness and disappointment: 'Vous n'avez rien compris à ma simplicité,' as he lamented. In the case of my friend there was, however, a sort of virginal devotion, as to a Madonna; and I think had things gone happily, to a conventionally happy ending, he would have felt (dare I say?) that his ideal had been spoilt.

But, for the good fortune of poets, things never do go happily with them, or to conventionally happy endings. So the wilder wanderings began, and a gradual slipping into deeper and steadier waters of oblivion. That curious love of the sordid, so common an affectation of the modern decadent, and with him so expressively genuine, grew upon him, and dragged him into yet more sorry corners of a life which was never exactly 'gay' to him. And now, indifferent to most things, in the shipwrecked quietude of a sort of self exile, he is living, I believe, somewhere on a remote foreign sea-coast. People will complain, probably, in his verses, of what will seem to them the factitious melancholy, the factitious idealism, and (peeping through at a few rare moments) the factitious suggestions of riot. They will see only a literary affectation where in truth there is as poignant a note of personal sincerity as in the more explicit and arranged confessions of less admirable poets. Yes, in these few, evasive, immaterial snatches of song, I find, implied for the most part, hidden away like a secret, all the fever and turmoil and the unattained dreams of a life which has itself had much of the swift, disastrous, and suicidal energy of genius.

'The Epitaph in Form of a Ballade Which Villon Made for Himself and His Companions When Expecting to Be Hanged with Them' (1896)

FRANÇOIS VILLON,

translated by Theodore Wratislaw

This poem was published in issue six of the Savoy, *which by then was quickly going bankrupt. It would eke out two more issues before folding, but this epitaph relates to both the magazine and the 'tragic generation' itself.*

Brothers who yet are living, mortal men,
Speak not of us with wrath and bitter tongue,
Since if your souls for us are filled with pain
The more will God's grace fall your hearts among.
You see us here upon the gibbets hung:
The flesh that we too much did glorify

Has long been putrid and devoured: and dry
As dust and ashes now our bleached bones be.
Let no man then our hideous shapes decry,
But pray that God may show us all mercy.

Brothers, speak not, we pray you, with disdain
Of us poor five or six by law upstrung.
It is not every man who has his brain
Clear and well-seated, as has oft been sung.

Make ye then intercession for our wrong
To him whose death from Hell our souls did buy,
Saving us from the flames that never die,
That fresh may flow the fount of His pity.
We are dead : let none to vex our spirits try,
But pray that God may show us all mercy.

Our bodies have been washed and drenched by rain,
Dried up and blackened by the sun; a throng
Of ravens and of crows our eyes have ta'en

And pluckt the brows and beards whereto they clung.

Never are we at rest, forever swung
By every wind that shifts and passes by,
Pecked by the sharp beaks of the crow and pye
And dinted like a thimble, as you see,
Have naught to say to them that with us vie,
But pray that God may show us all mercy.

Prince Jesus, Lord who reignest in the sky,
Grant that to Hell's fierce mouth we draw not nigh:
Toward such a place no love or wish have we.
Men, mock not us because we hang so high,
But pray that God may show us all mercy.

'Dregs' (1899)

ERNEST DOWSON

A translation of Knut Hamsun's Hunger *was published in 1899 with an illustration of an emaciated man on the cover. Oscar Wilde took this hideous figure to be a 'horrible caricature of Ernest'. With overtones of Dorian Gray, Wilde wrote 'The picture of Hunger grows more like Ernest daily. I now hide it'. In his youth, the poet was renowned for his beauty, but within a year of* Hunger's *publication, he would die from chronic alcoholism, aged just thirty-two. It was a tragic end to an unhappy life.*

The fire is out, and spent the warmth thereof
(This is the end of every song man sings!)
The golden wine is drunk, the dregs remain,
Bitter as wormwood and as salt as pain;
And health and hope have gone the way of love
Into the drear oblivion of lost things.
Ghosts go along with us until the end;
This was a mistress, this, perhaps, a friend.
With pale, indifferent eyes, we sit and wait
For the dropt curtain and the closing gate:
This is the end of all the songs man sings.

'A Last Word' (1899)

ERNEST DOWSON

Let us go hence: the night is now at hand;
 The day is overworn, the birds all flown;
 And we have reaped the crops the gods have sown;
Despair and death; deep darkness o'er the land,
Broods like an owl; we cannot understand
 Laughter or tears, for we have only known
 Surpassing vanity: vain things alone
Have driven our perverse and aimless band.

Let us go hence, somewhither strange and cold,
 To Hollow Lands where just men and unjust
Find end of labour, where's rest for the old,
 Freedom to all from love and fear and lust.
Twine our torn hands! O pray the earth enfold
 Our life-sick hearts and turn them into dust.

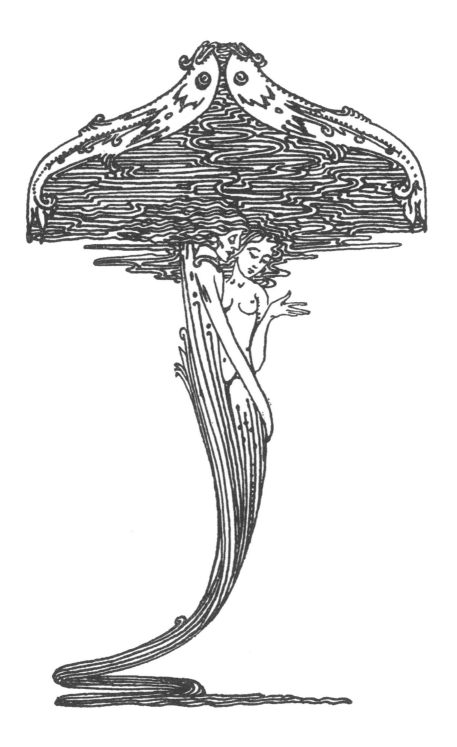

Author Biographies

John Barlas (1860–1914)

John Barlas was born in Burma and studied at New College, Oxford, where he befriended Oscar Wilde. He was an ardent socialist and an organiser for the Social Democratic Federation. In 1891 Barlas fired a revolver at the House of Commons out of contempt for Parliament, and was bailed out by Wilde following his arrest. He was briefly associated with the Rhymers' Club, under the sponsorship of Ernest Dowson. During the early 1890s he produced volumes of decadent verse under his own name and the pseudonym Evelyn Douglas. His mental health was fragile, and he spent much of his later life in Gartnavel Asylum in Glasgow.

Aubrey Beardsley (1872–1898)

Beardsley battled with tuberculosis from the age of nine and succumbed to the disease aged just twenty-five. It is odd to begin a biographical note with the subject's death, but rarely does the end loom so large over a person's life. Aware of the possibility of early death, he was a prolific artist in the time he had, and produced some of the most grotesque, and the most beautiful, images of the era. In 1896 he was made artistic director of the *Savoy*, in 1897 he converted to Roman Catholicism, and in 1898 he died in Menton, France. He was considered a musical prodigy as a child and gave piano concerts aged eleven.

William Beckford (1760–1844)

A precocious child of a rich family, he received an extensive education. At the age of five he took music lessons from Mozart, who was only eight at the time. William Beckford's father was twice Lord Mayor of London, and owned several sugar plantations in Jamaica. When Beckford was ten, he inherited his father's fortune and became one of the richest individuals of the time. His extravagant twenty-first birthday lasted three days and fuelled rumours of decadent orgies and scandal. He had many interests but devoted his vast wealth, and considerable intellectual talents, to building the greatest private art collection of the nineteenth century. His fiction is imaginative and his criticism insightful, but he will be remembered mostly as the builder of the magnificent, and sadly lost, Fonthill Abbey.

Max Beerbohm (1872–1956)

Sir Henry Maximilian 'Max' Beerbohm was the youngest of nine children of a Lithuanian-born grain merchant. He met Wilde and other literary figures at Oxford and contributed to the *Yellow Book* while he was still an undergraduate. While at Oxford, he also started drawing caricatures of society figures, which won him popular acclaim. He cultivated a reputation as a wit and a dandy, and was employed as the drama critic for the *Saturday Review* from 1898 until 1910 when he relocated to Rapallo, Italy. His only novel, *Zuleika Dobson*, was published in 1911.

Edward Bulwer-Lytton (1803–1873)
Edward George Earle Lytton Bulwer-Lytton, 1st Baron Lytton, was an English novelist, poet, playwright and politician. He was a prolific writer and, briefly, the most popular novelist in Britain before he was eclipsed by Charles Dickens. He preceded the decadent generation by several decades, but his extravagant lifestyle and preoccupations with art, the occult and fashion inspired those that followed. *Pelham* (1828) effectively changed the way men dressed, and won him acclaim as a wit and a dandy. His esoteric works, such as *Zanoni* (1842), were important contributions to an evolving Victorian spirituality. He was made a peer in 1866.

Aleister Crowley (1875–1947)
Mountaineer, chess player, poet, philosopher, novelist, artist and mystic, Crowley fitted more into one lifetime than most can even dream of. In 1897 he met Leonard Smithers, publisher of the *Savoy*, and through him printed his first two volumes of poetry: *Aceldama, a Place to Bury Strangers in: A Philosophical Poem by a Gentleman of the University of Cambridge* (1898) and *White Stains* (1898). Crowley knew several of the decadent circle and fell out badly with W. B. Yeats. His literary output is voluminous and varied – in both subject and quality – but his libertine lifestyle was decadent in the extreme.

Olive Custance (1874–1944)
Olive Custance was a brilliant young poet who joined the London literary circle of Wilde, Dowson and Beardsley around 1890, aged just sixteen. She befriended Beardsley, who designed a bookplate for her, and contributed to the *Yellow Book*. In 1901 she lived in Paris, and had brief relationships with the writers Natalie Clifford Barney and Renée Vivien. That same year she began writing to Lord Alfred Douglas (Oscar Wilde's former lover) and the two married in 1902. The relationship was strained, with periods of separation, but they remained married until death, and died within a year of each other. She had several volumes of verse published, and continued to write throughout her lifetime.

Ernest Dowson (1867–1900)
The quintessential decadent poet, Ernest Dowson lived a short life marked by tragedy, depression and intoxication, but produced some of the most impressive work of the period. He gave us such famous phrases as 'They are not long, the days of wine and roses' and 'gone with the wind', although few have ever heard of the man who coined them. He also wrote 'absinthe makes the tart grow fonder', and provides the earliest written usage of the word soccer to refer to football (spelled 'soca'; a reference to Association Football). His other major contribution was the translation of French works including *Les Liaisons Dangereuses*. He attended the

Queen's College, Oxford, but left without obtaining a degree. In London he attended the Rhymers' Club, where he was considered one of the club's strongest talents. In 1889 he fell in love with the eleven-year-old daughter of a Polish restaurant owner. His infatuation lasted years and he was devastated when she refused his proposal and married somebody else. In 1891 he converted to Catholicism. In 1894 both his parents committed suicide. His own health declined shortly afterwards and he spent much of the rest of his life in France, before returning to England, destitute and alcoholic, to die of tuberculosis aged thirty-two.

Michael Field

'Michael Field' was the pen name adopted by Katherine Bradley (1846–1914) and her niece Edith Cooper (1862–1913). Katherine adopted and raised Edith after her mother fell ill. At some point in Edith's teenage years they became lovers. 'The Michael Fields', as they were known to their friends, knew many of the literary figures of the 1880s and 1890s, but tried to keep their true identity secret from the public. Katherine was briefly a member of John Ruskin's utopian society, the Guild of Saint George, although he ended the friendship after she announced that she had lost God and found a dog. They were active in the anti-vivisection movement and were strong supporters of women's suffrage. After living a sort of Arcadian paganism, they converted to Catholicism in 1906. They died within a year of each other. In their lifetimes they published twenty-seven plays and eight volumes of poetry, although they are largely forgotten today.

Richard Le Gallienne (1866–1947)

The son of a brewery manager, Richard Thomas Gallienne was born in Liverpool. He was briefly apprenticed to a firm of accountants, before changing his name and leaving for London in 1889. He was one of the most distinctive 'Men of the Nineties', growing his hair long and dressing flamboyantly. He became a reader for John Lane's Bodley Head publishing house, contributed to the *Yellow Book* and the *Savoy*, and associated with the Rhymers' Club. He wrote prolifically, and his memoir, *The Romantic '90s* (1925) is an interesting account of the period. He moved to America in 1905 and then France in the 1940s. He is buried in Menton, near Aubrey Beardsley.

Sir Edmund Gosse (1849–1928)

Like Aleister Crowley, Edmund Gosse was brought up in a strict Plymouth Brethren sect – and, like Crowley, he broke away from it in his adolescence. His autobiography *Father and Son* (1907) recounts this coming of age, and is considered a classic of the genre. At eighteen Gosse found work at the British Museum as an assistant librarian. He later lectured in English Literature at Cambridge, and by the 1890s was renowned as a man of letters. He wrote several volumes of poetry, but was more influential as a critic, translator and literary socialite. He helped introduce Henrik Ibsen, W. B. Yeats and James Joyce to the British public. In 1925 he was knighted.

John Gray (1866–1934)

John Gray was born in Bethnal Green to a working-class family, leaving school at thirteen to become an apprentice metal-worker. Possessing a keen intellect, however, he continued his education through evening classes and fell in with the nascent aesthetic crowd. In 1889 he met Oscar Wilde for the first time. The specifics of their relationship are conjectural, but the young and beautiful John Gray was almost certainly the model for Dorian Gray. They had an intense relationship in the early Nineties, and John Gray became known as 'Dorian' in their literary circle. He published his first volume of poetry, *Silverpoints*, in 1893. In 1890 he was baptised as a Roman Catholic, but almost immediately lapsed. He rediscovered his faith in 1895, was ordained in 1901, and spent the rest of his life serving as a priest in Edinburgh.

J. K. Huysmans (1848–1907)

Joris-Karl Huysmans worked as a civil servant in France for most of his life, while writing in his spare time. In 1884 he published *À Rebours* (*Against Nature*), a book about a weary aesthete who retires from the world to live in an artificial paradise. It inspired a generation. Arthur Symons wrote of Huysmans, 'Elaborately and deliberately perverse, it is in its very perversity that Huysmans' work – so fascinating, so repellent, so instinctively artificial – comes to represent, as the work of no other writer can be said to do, the main tendencies, the chief results, of the Decadent movement in literature.' The book is referenced obliquely in *Dorian Gray*, and was used as evidence against Wilde in his trial. In 1892 Huysmans returned to the Catholic church and in 1900 became an oblate at a Benedictine monastery.

Lionel Johnson (1867–1902)

Johnson was born in Kent, and educated at Winchester College and New College, Oxford. In 1890 he graduated and moved into the 'Fitzroy Settlement', the property at Fitzroy Street, London, that was the home, offices and studios of the Century Guild of Artists. He began a career as a journalist and associated with many literary figures of the age. He converted to Catholicism in 1891 and considered taking orders. From 1895 he became increasingly withdrawn, struggling with alcoholism and his repressed homosexuality. His tortured verse perhaps best captures a longing for salvation, expressed through religious sentiment and decadent themes. In 1902 he died of a stroke after a fall. In some tellings, it was after a fall in the street, in others, it was said to be a fall from a barstool.

Ada Leverson (1862–1933)

Ada Leverson began writing in the 1880s, contributing to numerous periodicals of the day, including *Punch* and the *Yellow Book*. She gained a reputation as a wit, and was known for her satirical writings about culture and high society. Oscar Wilde called her 'the wittiest woman in the world', nicknamed her 'the Sphinx', and helped grow her career. She remained a loyal friend to Wilde when others abandoned him, even allowing him to stay at her home when he was released on bail from his criminal trial. She wrote less as she aged, but maintained a large literary circle and encouraged writers of the next generation, such as Somerset Maugham, T. S. Eliot and Percy Wyndham Lewis.

Arthur Machen (1863–1947)

Arthur Machen came from a long line of Welsh clergymen. His father was an Anglican priest who baptised him as Arthur Llewellyn Jones, and he was raised in the rectory of Llandewi, near Caerleon. He was a solitary child who became fascinated with the sublime landscape of Monmouthshire and its Celtic and Roman history. In the 1870s local archaeologists discovered a series of statues and Roman inscriptions in the area. These strange pagan relics made a deep impression on Machen and his later fiction. His first major success was *The Great God Pan*, published in John Lane's *Keynotes* series in 1894. He was seen by the public as a writer of 'Decadent horror', an appellation that's not entirely accurate and which probably did more harm than good in the post-Wilde scandal years. Machen supplemented his income from fiction with work as a journalist and saw his fortunes rise and fall several times over his lifetime. His impact on modern gothic fiction is substantial and, since his death, his reputation has grown deservedly.

Vincent O'Sullivan (1868–1940)

An American who moved to Britain in his childhood, O'Sullivan was a short-story writer obsessed with morbid, decadent and Gothic themes. In 1897 he published the collection *Houses of Sin*, featuring a cover design by Aubrey Beardsley. In 1907 his brother lost the family fortune, and he was made destitute for the rest of his life. He died in Paris.

Walter Pater (1839–1894)

Walter Pater was a quiet and thoughtful Oxford academic, who nevertheless became one of the most influential theorists behind aestheticism and decadence. His *Studies in the History of the Renaissance* (1873) seems tame to modern readers but was controversial on publication for its 'Conclusion', which seemed to suggest that earthly experience is more important than heavenly reward. This eloquent appeal to live a life of exquisite sensation became a bible for those inclined towards such things. At Oxford he befriended and encouraged many brilliant undergraduates who sought him out, inspired by his writings. Arthur Symons and Oscar Wilde were among his acolytes.

Thomas De Quincey (1785–1859)

Thomas De Quincey was a gifted but sickly child. In his adolescence he suffered periods of depression, and was consoled by the works of Wordsworth and Coleridge. He attended Oxford, where he first used opium, but did not graduate. He later began an uneven literary career as a journalist. His life was marked by financial and medical trouble, and it was against this backdrop that his opium addiction deepened. *Confessions of an English Opium-Eater* won him literary fame overnight and, despite the moments of horror he described, enticed many more to the drug. It is the seminal book of addiction literature.

M. P. Shiel (1865–1947)

Matthew Phipps Shiell was born on the island of Montserrat in the West Indies. He moved to England in 1885, dropped the second 'l' from his surname, and began a career as a writer. He had several short stories published in the *Strand* and the *Pall Mall Magazine*, and published two decadent collections in John Lane's *Keynotes* series: *Prince Zaleski* in 1895 and *Shapes in the Fire* in 1896. Although he wrote prolifically, most of his reputation rests on his future history novel *The Purple Cloud*, written in 1901.

Count Eric Stanislaus Stenbock (1860–1895)

A Baltic aristocrat and poet – memorably described by W. B. Yeats as 'Scholar, connoisseur, drunkard, poet, pervert, most charming of men' – Count Stenbock is certainly one of the strangest figures in this anthology. He produced very little work (what exists is now incredibly rare), but lived one of the most eccentric and decadent lives of them all. He attended Balliol, Oxford, where he tried a different religion every week, but did not complete his studies. In the garden of his ancestral home in Estonia he had a small zoo comprising a fox, a bear and a few reindeer, and he kept snakes and lizards in the house. He later evolved his own syncretic religion, and carried everywhere with him a wooden doll that he referred to as 'le petit comte' and believed to be his son. By the 1890s he had descended into alcohol and opium addiction, and moved to his mother's house in Brighton. He died during a drunken argument with his stepfather, when he fell onto the fireplace.

Arthur Symons (1865–1945)

Born in Wales and privately educated (his father was a Methodist minister), Symons as a young man broke away from his family and frequently travelled to France, where he fell in love with the country and its writers, meeting and befriending many of the leading lights. In 1895 he shared a flat at Fountain Court, London, with W. B. Yeats. He contributed poems and essays to the *Yellow Book* before assuming editorship of the *Savoy* in 1896. The magazine was conceived in Dieppe, and much of the material of the first two issues was written or edited in France. Symons played a major role in connecting the artistic scenes of the two countries. On a trip through Italy in 1908 he suffered a nervous breakdown, which required two years of hospitalisation. He never truly recovered, although he carried on writing until his death.

Oscar Wilde (1854–1900)

The son of middle-class Dublin intellectuals, Oscar Wilde received an excellent education and was fluent in French and German as a child. His formidable talents won him a scholarship to Oxford, where he was tutored by John Ruskin and Walter Pater. Here he began to cultivate a self-consciously aesthetic style, which won him a reputation that extended beyond the university and into the public consciousness. He wore his hair long, dressed flamboyantly and dispensed epigrams that made him famous. *Punch* caricatured him while he was still a student. It is interesting to note that at this point Oscar Wilde had written practically nothing of importance, but was becoming famous simply for being Oscar Wilde. In 1882 his fame was sufficient that he embarked on a year-long lecture tour of America, discussing the Aesthetic movement. Literary success came with *The Picture of Dorian Gray* (1891) and *The Importance of Being Earnest* (1895). In 1895 a scandalous court case, and subsequent two-year prison term, ruined him financially and physically, and he died in 1900.

Theodore Wratislaw (1871–1933)

Theodore Wratislaw was born in Rugby, and attended Ruby School, where his great-grandfather and great-uncle had been masters. He also had a legitimate claim to be a Count of Bohemia and a Count of the Holy Roman Empire; his family was descended from the founder of the city of Prague and held the title of Count Wratislavia before their emigration to Britain three generations previously. He trained as a solicitor after leaving school, but decided instead on a literary career and moved to London where he fell in with Wilde, Beardsley and Symons. He published two volumes of decadent verse, *Caprices* (1893) and the excellent *Orchids* (1896), and contributed to both the *Yellow Book* and the *Savoy*. Despite his bohemian aristocratic lineage Wratislaw did not live a particularly decadent life, and gave up writing in 1895 to enter the civil service. If remembered at all, he is generally considered a minor figure in the Decadent movement, although a blue plaque at his old house in Surrey commemorates that 'Count Theodore Wratislaw' once lived there.

W. B. Yeats (1865–1939)

Now regarded as one of the greatest poets of the twentieth century, W. B. Yeats spent his formative years on the fringes of the Decadent movement. His career accelerated at an incredible pace after breaking free, but it was during those years that he founded the Rhymers' Club, met Lady Gregory (who became his lifelong friend and patron), and explored his occult interests through joining the Golden Dawn society. He was later a driving force behind the Irish Literary Revival, and in 1923 he was awarded the Nobel Prize in Literature.

List of Illustrations

p.84 'The Bard of Beauty', caricature of Oscar Wilde. (Eccles Bequest)

p.88 Illustration by Harry Clarke, Geoffrey Warren, *Elixir of Life*, 1925. (08234.de.3)

p.90 'The Absinthe Drinker' by Felicien Rop, Érastène Ramiro, *Felicien Rops*, 1905. (K.T.C.27.a.23)

p.99 'Absinthe Robette', poster design by Privat Livemont, 1896. Maurice Bauwens, *Les Affiches* étrangères *illustrées*, 1897. (7856.g.22)

p.100 Aubrey Beardsley self-portrait. Aubrey Beardsley, *A Second Book of Fifty Drawings*, 1899. (K.T.C.37.b.16)

p.113 Illustration from *The Savoy*, no.5, 1896. (K.T.C.35.a.14)

p.117 Illustration by Harry Clarke, Geoffrey Warren, *Elixir of Life*, 1925. (08234.de.3)

p.120 'Giving heed to seducing spirits', illustration by William T. Horton, *The Savoy*, no.2, 1896. (K.T.C.35.a.14)

p.124 Illustration by Harry Clarke, Algernon Charles Swinburne, *Selected Poems*, 1928. (11643.n.15)

p.133 'They have sharpened their tongues like a serpent; adders poison is under their lips', illustration by William T. Horton, *The Savoy*, no.2, 1896. (K.T.C.35.a.14)

p.137 Illustration by E. Couboin, Edmond Haraucourt, *L'Antéchrist*, 1894. (Tab.502.b.9)

p.141 'The Dwellers on the Threshold' illustration by Austin Osman Spare, Austin Osman Spare, *Earth. Inferno*, 1905. (1870.a.11)

p.142 Portion of a Japanese stencil plate, *The Studio*, vol.2, 1894. (P.P.1931.pcu)

p.146 Illustration by Sidney H. Sime, Baron Dunsany, *Time & the Gods*, 1922. (L.R.408.c.7)

p.152 Illustration by Harry Clarke, Algernon Charles Swinburne, *Selected Poems*, 1928. (11643.n.15_)

p.157 'I saw them march From Dover, long ago', illustration by Harry Clarke, L. D'Oyley Walters, *The Year's at the Spring. An anthology of recent poetry*, 1920. (11603.h.21)

p.160 William T. Horton, *A Book of Images*, 1898. (L.R.269.a.2/2)

p.162 Illustration by Auguste Lepère, J. K. Huysmans, *A Rebours*, 1903. (C.108.gg.2)

p.165 Illustration by Aubrey Beardsley, Oscar Wilde, *Salome. A Tragedy in One Act*, 1894. (Eccles 296)

p.167 *The Yellow Book*, vol.1, 1893. (Eccles 1085)

p.168 Illustration by Carlos Schwabe, Edmond Haraucourt, *L'Effort*, 1894. (Tab.502.b.9)

p.170 Illustration by Alastair, Harry Crosby, *Red Skeletons*, 1927. (Cup.310.fa.1)

p.177 Illustration by Alastair, Harry Crosby, *Red Skeletons*, 1927. (Cup.310.fa.1)

p.179 Illustration by Aubrey Beardsley, *The Savoy*, no.3, 1896. (K.T.C.35.a.14)

p.182 Illustration by William T. Horton, *The Savoy*, no.7. 1896. (K.T.C.35.a.14)

Acknowledgements

Many thanks to the following people, who helped bring this book into existence: Alice Wright for her early encouragement, Rob Davies for commissioning the book, Sally Nicholls for her excellent picture research (and putting up with my many requests), my wonderful editor Miranda Harrison for her calm approach and her commitment to making the book the best it could be, and Briony Hartley for her beautiful design work.

First published in 2017 by
The British Library
96 Euston Road
London NW1 2DB

Introduction and notes © 2017 Jon Crabb

British Library Cataloguing-in-Publication Data
A catalogue record for this book is available from the British Library

ISBN: 978-0-7123-5663-3

Designed and typeset by Briony Hartley, Goldust Design
Picture research by Sally Nicholls
Printed in the Czech Republic by PB Tisk